Beacon Small-Group Bible Studies

Psalms

Beacon Small-Group Bible Studies

PSALMS

Keeping the Heart Aglow

by
Ivan A. Beals

Beacon Hill Press of Kansas City
Kansas City, Missouri

Copyright 1984
by Beacon Press of Kansas City

ISBN: 0-8341-0885-2 (The Psalms)

ISBN: 0-8341-0624-8 (Set)

Printed in the United States of America

Cover photo: C. S. Jenkins, courtesy of Lorraine Schultz.

Permission to quote from the following copyrighted versions of the Bible is acknowledged with appreciation:

New American Standard Bible (NASB), © The Lockman Foundation, 1960, 1962, 1963, 1968, 1971, 1972, 1973, 1975, 1977.

The Holy Bible, New International Version (NIV), copyright © 1978 by New York International Bible Society.

Revised Standard Version of the Bible (RSV), copyrighted 1946, 1952, © 1971, 1973.

The Bible: A New Translation (Moffatt), copyrighted 1954 by James A. R. Moffatt. By permission of Harper and Row, Publishers, Inc.

Modern Language Bible, the *New Berkeley Version in Modern English* (NBV), copyright © 1945, 1959, 1969 by Zondervan Publishing House.

Unless otherwise noted, all Scripture quotations are from the NIV.

Unless otherwise noted, all hymn quotations in this study guide are from the 1878 edition of the *Hymnal of the Methodist Episcopal Church*. The major portion of the hymns in this hymnal were composed by John and Charles Wesley.

10 9 8 7 6 5 4 3 2

Contents

How to Use This Study Guide		6
Introduction		11
1	**Contrasting Portraits**—Psalm 1	13
2	**The Glory of God's Work and Word**—Psalm 19	19
3	**The Sob and the Song**—Psalm 22	25
4	**The Lord as Shepherd and Host**—Psalm 23	31
5	**Worship the King of Glory**—Psalm 24	37
6	**Don't Worry—Trust God**—Psalm 37	42
7	**The Soul's Thirst for God**—Psalms 42 and 43	48
8	**Plea for Pardon and Purity**—Psalm 51	54
9	**The Riddle of Life**—Psalm 73	59
10	**Heart Hunger for God's House**—Psalm 84	65
11	**Refuge for the Trusting Heart**—Psalm 91	70
12	**A Full Heart Sings Praises**—Psalm 103	75
13	**The Traveler's Psalms**—Psalms 121 and 122	80
14	**God, the Searcher of Hearts**—Psalm 139	85
15	**Praise the Lord**—Psalms 148; 149; and 150	90
Bibliography		96

HOW TO USE THIS STUDY GUIDE

Before You Begin This Adventure in a Small-Group Bible Study... Read These Pages of Introduction

God has created us with a basic human need for close personal relationships. This may take place *as you gather in a small group* to apply the Bible to your life.

I. What Should Happen in Small-Group Bible Study?

"They devoted themselves to the apostles' teaching and to the fellowship... and to prayer" (Acts 2:42, NIV).

Each group is different... yet all should include three kinds of activity—
DISCUSSION BIBLE STUDY
SHARING EXPERIENCES
PRAYING TOGETHER

The time you spend in Bible study, sharing, and praying will vary according to the needs of the group. However, do not neglect any of these activities.

The Bible contains God's plan for our salvation and gives us His guidance for our lives. Keep the focus on God speaking to you from His Word.

On the other hand, just to learn "Bible facts" will make little difference in a person's life. To give opportunity for persons to *share* what the truth means to them is to "let God come alive today." Learn to listen intently to others and to share what you feel God's Word is saying to you.

Allow time for *prayer*. Personal communion with God is essential in all fruitful Bible studies. Determine to make prayer more than a "nod to God" at the beginning or end of each session. As members participate in sincere, unhurried prayer—you will be amazed how God's power will meet needs in your group... today!

II. How to Begin Your First Session Together

The leader of a new group may wish to prepare name tags with first and last names large enough to be seen plainly.

It is important to order the *Beacon Small-Group Bible Study* guides and give one to each person in your group at the beginning of the first session. Pass out the guides and refer the group to this section of the Introduction. Then ask each person to consider the following:

One thing I would like to gain from sharing in this time together is:

Rank the following in order using number one (1) to indicate the most important and number five (5) the least important.

( ) 1. Learning to know Bible truths and apply them to my life.
( ) 2. A chance to begin all over again in my spiritual life.
( ) 3. To grow in my personal faith in God.
( ) 4. To deepen my friendships with others in the group as we study the Word together.
( ) 5. Other purpose _____

Take time to go around the group to introduce yourselves. Then let each member share what he or she would like to gain from this Bible study by filling in the blanks and by discussing this statement: I chose _____ as number one because _____. I put _____ as number five because _____.

At this point, pause for prayer, asking God to bless this Bible study and especially to meet the needs just expressed by the members of the group.

III. A Key to Success... Make a Group Commitment

What should be included in the group commitment? At the first or second meeting, read the following points, then discuss each one separately.

1. Agree to make regular attendance a top priority of the group.
   Commitment to each other is of vital importance.

2. Where and when will the group meet?
   Decide on a place and time. The place can be always in the same home or in a different home each week, at a restaurant, or in any other relaxed setting. Plan to be on time.
   The time _____ the place(s) _____
   How often?   ( ) Every week
                 ( ) Every other week

3. Decide on the length of the meetings.
   The minimum should be one hour—maximum two hours. Whatever you decide, be sure to dismiss on time. Those who wish may remain after the group is dismissed. Length _____.

4. Decide whether the same person will lead each session, or if you prefer a group coordinator and a rotation of leaders.

   Our leader or coordinator is _____.

5. Agree together that there shall be no criticism of others. Also no discussion of church problems, and no gossip shall be expressed in the group. Our goal in this Bible study is to affirm and to build up each other.

6. Decide on the maximum number of people your group should contain. When this number is reached you will encourage the formation of a new group. We want our group to grow. Newcomers, as they understand and agree to the group commitment, will keep things fresh. Feel free to bring a

friend. Whenever our group reaches an average attendance of _____ persons for three consecutive weeks, we will plan to begin a new group.

Do not become a closed clique. This would eventually lead to an ingrown group. Our goal is outreach, friendliness, and openness to new people.

7. Our time together as a group will be more fulfilling if all of us complete our personal Bible reading before we come together again.

    Are group members deciding to make this commitment to personal Bible reading and reflection? _____

8. Decide on the number of times you wish to meet before you reevaluate the areas of your commitment. (Enter below)

**MY COMMITMENT TO CHRIST
and THE MEMBERS OF MY GROUP**

I agree to meet with others in my group for _____ weeks to become a learner in God's Word.

I commit myself to give priority to our group gatherings, to a thoughtful reading of the Bible passages to be explored, and to love and support others in my group.

Signed _____ Date _____

IV. Guidelines

1. Get acquainted with each other; get on a first-name basis.
2. Each one bring your Bible and keep it open during the study.
3. As you read the Bible passage, each person may ask himself three questions:
    —What does the passage say?
    —What does it mean?
    —What does it mean to me?
4. Stay with the Bible passage before you. Moving to numerous cross references may confuse a person new to the Bible.
5. Avoid technical theological words. Make sure any theological terms you use are explained clearly to the group.
6. The leader or coordinator should prepare for each session by studying the passage thoroughly before the group meeting, including reviewing the

HOW TO USE THIS STUDY GUIDE

questions in the study guide. In the group study, the leader should ask the study guide questions, giving adequate time for the discussion of each question.

Remember, the leader is not to lecture on what he has learned from studying, but should lead the group in discovering for themselves what the scripture says. In sharing your discoveries say, "The scripture says," rather than, "My church says..."

7. The leader should not talk too much and should not answer his own questions. The leader should give opportunity for anyone who wishes to speak. Redirect some of the questions back to the group. As they get to know each other better, the discussion will move more freely.

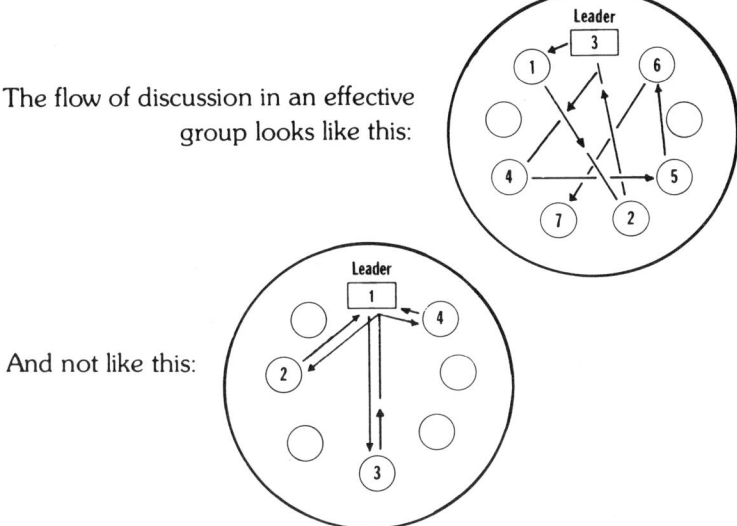

The flow of discussion in an effective group looks like this:

And not like this:

8. In a loving and firm manner maintain the guidelines for the group. Discourage overtalkative members from monopolizing the time. If necessary, the leader may speak privately to the overtalkative one and enlist his aid in encouraging all to participate. Direct questions to all persons in the group.

9. Plan to reserve some time at the end of each session for prayer together. Encourage any who wish to lead out in spoken prayer in response to the scripture truths or personal needs expressed in the group.

Even if you do not complete all the study for that particular meeting, *take time to pray*. The main purpose of group Bible study is not just to cover all the facts, but to apply the truth to human lives. It will be exciting to discover your lives growing and changing as you encourage each other in Christ's love.

A highly effective way to pray in a group like this is "conversationally." "Conversational" prayer includes:
  a. Each group member who wishes to do so tells God frankly what he has to say to Him.
  b. Praying is in a conversational tone—directly, simply, briefly.
  c. Only one thing is prayed about at a time—a personal concern.
  d. Once a group member has introduced his concern, at least one other member, and probably several, by audible prayer "covers with love" their friend's concern.
  e. Then there is a waiting in silence before God. Each person listens to what God is saying to him.
  f. Following the listening period, another member may introduce a personal concern in prayer. The prayer time continues with members feeling free to pray several times.

V. Aids for Your Study
For Group Leaders
You will find helpful *How to Lead a Small-Group Bible Study,* by Gene Van Note, available from the Beacon Hill Press of Kansas City, Box 527, Kansas City, MO 64141.

This study guide suggests frequent use of unison reading and responsive scripture readings. For these periods you will need enough copies of one version of the Bible for the entire group to participate. If you are to repeat common passages from memory, you will also need to work from the same version.

For Leaders, Coordinators, and Participants
Bible commentaries should not be taken with you to the study period, but it is often helpful to refer to sound commentaries and expositions in your preparation. We recommend:
> *Beacon Bible Commentary*
>   Volume 3—Job—Song of Solomon
> *Adam Clarke's Commentary on the Entire Bible:*
>   One-Volume Edition

It is also helpful to refer occasionally to some general Bible resources, such as:
> *Know Your Old Testament,* by W. T. Purkiser
> *Halley's Bible Handbook*

The above resources are available from Beacon Hill Press of Kansas City or from your publishing house.

—This Introduction by Wil M. Spaite

About Psalms

Happiness is—singing God's praises! The psalms are truly "heart-warmers," revealing divine truth.

The Hebrew title of the Book of Psalms, *Tehillim,* means "praises" or "songs of praise." Our English title is from the Greek Septuagint translation, made about 150 B.C. *Psalmoi,* the Greek term, means "songs" or "sacred songs." It is derived from a root that means to "touch," as of the chords of a stringed instrument.

The Psalms have been described as "the grandest symphony of praise to God ever composed on earth" (*Beacon Bible Commentary,* 3:127). David and others who authored these hymns used a lyre to accompany their singing. But no harp or other musical instrument is needed to profit from their study.

Although the Psalter is called the Hymnbook of the Hebrews, our hymns differ in one respect from these psalms. In our hymns the music is stirred by the words. The word "psalm," however, means a composition set to music. The art of sweeping the strings, called "psalming," inspired the poems. The words were thus stirred by music.

This Hebrew religious poetry is lyrical in character and parallel in form. It doesn't follow rhyme, but rather rhythm. Looking for rhythmic, repeated thoughts, our appreciation and interpretation of a psalm is enhanced.

These sacred songs are divided into five books:

      Book I   Psalms 1—41
      Book II   Psalms 42—72
      Book III   Psalms 73—89
      Book IV   Psalms 90—106
      Book V   Psalms 107—150

The psalms bathe Israel's history in the sunlight of religious devotion and spiritual fervor; they all rise from personal experience, as the Spirit of God inspired the writers. Martin Luther spoke of the Book of Psalms as "a Bible in miniature."

The Lord God of the Psalms provides the glowing warmth of life to all who meditate on them. Placing ourselves and our experiences in a psalm, we join the community of the saints. Repeating their words in faith, we may sing the same song.

Of the 150 psalms, 100 are related to authors by their titles. Of these, 73 are assigned to David, 12 to the School of Asaph, 10 to the School of Korah, 2 to Solomon, 1 to Ethan, 1 to Heman, 1 to Moses, and 50 are anonymous.

David's writings are the foundation of the Psalter. He was a gifted musician and lyric poet, founding a new era of religious expression. It was he who originated the Temple liturgy (1 Chronicles 25). A man of fervent religious experience, David reveals his deep feelings with vivid imagery. He ever seeks the Divine Presence.

A major portion of the Psalms (Books I—III) are thought to have originated 1000 to 700 B.C., from David to Hezekiah. The rest (Books IV—V) probably belong to the exilic and postexilic periods, up to the time of Nehemiah, around 445-435 B.C.

Our sampler study involves 15 lessons on 19 psalms, representing each of the five books. These include Psalms 1; 19; 22; 23; 24; 37; 42—43; 51; 73; 84; 91; 103; 121—122; 139; and 148—150. Herein, the writers express the doubts, fears, hopes, joys, longings, gratitude, and praise of generations of pious people. They reveal the pulse of tested believers.

As John Wesley notes, the Book of Psalms "draws us off from converse with men, with the thinkers of this world, and directs us into communion with God" (*Explanatory Notes upon the Old Testament,* 2:1625).

Let us join in the multi-toned voice of prayer, addressing God in confession, petition, intercession, meditation, thanksgiving, and praise, both in public and in private. As we do, our hearts will come aglow with a fresh knowledge of God's presence, love, and care.

1 Contrasting Portraits

PSALM 1

Life on earth is sometimes pictured as a double exposure, a mixture of right and wrong. The Scriptures, however, clearly show some vivid contrasts.

In Psalm 1 an anonymous author exalts God's Word. He voices a serious call to a study of the book and of all the Holy Scriptures. This first psalm is a prelude to the whole five-book collection. The 41 psalms of Book I are all ascribed to David except Psalms 1; 2; 10; and 33, which are untitled.

Psalm 1 is classified as a wisdom psalm, with true happiness as the theme. Two contrasting portraits are drawn. A sharp distinction is shown between the righteous and the wicked, a common theme in wisdom literature. A doctrine of rewards is set forth: The righteous prosper and are happy; the wicked are troubled and short-lived. The Hebrews believed in God's righteous government, despite all appearances to the contrary. The righteous are blessed and the wicked are cursed—finally. This fact is the subject of Psalm 1.

Outline
I. The Blessings of the Righteous (1:1-3)
II. The Tragedy of the Ungodly (1:4-5)
III. Summary (1:6)

After some moments of silent prayer, begin your study by asking someone to read Psalm 1 aloud from the *New International Version*. You may also want to read it from the King James or other versions.

Besides being both a prayer book and a hymnbook to Jews and Christians, the Psalms have inspired the writing of many Christian hymns. Compare two verses based on Psalm 1:

Delight in the Bible

When quiet in my house I sit
  Thy book be my companion still;
My joy thy sayings to repeat,
  Talk o'er the records of thy will,
And search the oracles divine,
Till every heart-felt word be mine.

O may the gracious words divine,
  Subject of all my converse be;
So will the Lord his follower join,
  And walk and talk himself with me:
So shall my heart his presence prove,
And burn with everlasting love.

—Charles Wesley

I. The Blessings of the Righteous (Read 1:1-3)

A pleasant portrait is shown. The godly man is "blessed"—"happy" (v. 1). In the Hebrew, the word "blessed" is plural. There is no such thing as a single blessing. Wherever there is one, there are others. Compare the Beatitudes given by Jesus (Matt. 5:3-11).

A. Avoid Evil (v. 1)

The righteous man is happy in what he does not do. Religion is more than the "thou shalt nots," but certain God-given restraints govern our relationships.

1. List three things a godly man will not do.
    a. *to steal*
    b. *to*
    c. *to*

Note the three sets of triplets in verse 1:
  "walk—stand—sit"
  "counsel—way—seat"
  "wicked—sinners—mockers"

2. Write out the successive steps to a career of evil.
    a. _____
    b. _____
    c. _____

3. Do you agree with John Wesley who said that the sinners in Scripture are worse than the ungodly (KJV); and the scornful mockers are the worst of sinners? Yes ____ No ____

4. A Hebrew notion included in the meaning of "wicked" suggests unrest. How does our relationship to God influence our rest and unrest?

_____

5. Show how the Old Testament evils parallel some modern forms we face.

Old Testament Evils	Modern Forms
a. Walk in counsel of the wicked	a. _____
b. Stand with sinners	b. _____
c. Sit with mockers	c. _____

6. Are the ultimate choices in life clear-cut? Discuss with the group.

B. Delight in God (v. 2)

The secret of a life acceptable to God is to delight, to meditate, and to continue in the law of the Lord. The Hebrew term *torah* has a more precise meaning than is suggested by our word "law." It refers to the whole revealed way of life contained in the teachings of Moses and the prophets.

1. What is the blessed man's attitude toward God's will for his life?

_____

2. How does one delight in God's law as his rule of life? _____

_____

3. How do I respond to the "law of the Lord"—both the commandments and the personal convictions God has given me? (1) Accept them grudgingly ____ (2) Thank God for them ____ (3) Other attitude ____

4. Read Matt. 22:37-40. Is my life controlled by this law of love? Yes ____ No ____

5. How do you think the response of Christians today should compare to the faith of Old Testament believers? _____

	Same/Different
a. Truth	a. Fuller revelation
b. Obedience	b. _____
c. Sacrifice	c. _____
d. Hope	d. _____
e. Worship	e. _____

C. Like a Tree (v. 3)
1. In how many ways is the life of the righteous like a tree? What do the following words suggest to you?
   a. Planted—_____
   b. Streams—_____
   c. Fruit—_____
   d. Leaf—_____
   e. Prospers—_____
2. Does such prosperity refer only to material gain? Yes ___ No ___
3. In what other ways may prosperity refer to qualities of life?
   a. _____
   b. _____

II. The Tragedy of the Ungodly (Read 1:4-5)

The profile of the ungodly is given in sad terms. Rather than green trees, they are dry, useless chaff—hulls beaten from wheat, the discard of threshing. A tree withstands the storm, but the chaff is driven before it.

A. "Not so the wicked!" (v. 4)
1. Circle the following statements true or false.
   T F The ungodly are utterly unstable and insecure.
   T F The wind of verse 4 represents the judgment of God.
2. Contrast the ways wicked lives differ from righteous lives as shown in verses 3-4.

Righteous	Chaff
a. Root	a. _____
b. Fruit	b. _____
c. Leaf	c. _____

B. Judgment of God (v. 5)
1. Those who stand in the way of sinners (v. 1) shall not stand in the judgment. How do the decisions of life affect one's destiny? _____

2. Do you think there is a present judgment as well as final future judgment against evildoers? Yes ___ No ___

3. Give some reasons why the pleasures of the wicked are short-lived:

1 / CONTRASTING PORTRAITS

      a. _____

      b _____

  4. What do you think is meant by "the assembly of the righteous"? _____

III. Summary (Read 1:6)

A. "The Lord Watches Over the Way of the Righteous"

  1. In what manner does the Lord "know" (NASB) the righteous and protect his way? _____

  2. Write at least two ways in which our lives should be joined to the life of God, so that we may stand.

      a. _____

      b. _____

B. The Wicked Perish (cf. Prov. 14:12)

  1. W. Graham Scroggie supplies an ellipsis in verse 6—it reads:

> The Lord knoweth the way of the righteous,
> *Therefore it shall abide;*
> But the way of the ungodly shall perish,
> *For the Lord knoweth it not.*
>
> (With KJV; *The Psalter,* 1:10)

  2. Wesley notes that all the designs and courses of the wicked shall come to nothing, and the designs shall perish with the wicked. What do you think it means for the wicked to perish? _____

IV. Afterglow

  1. Though the scorner's seat is lofty, it is very near the gates of hell.

  2. Consider how God's law has brought growth in your spiritual life.

  3. Remember, only God can make sinners righteous. Share with the group what God has done for you.

V. Prayer Time

When you pray:

  1. Thank God for His watchcare throughout your life.

  2. Seek His continued guidance as you obey His will.

  3. Invite His presence to sustain you in the tempests of life.

4. Pray that you may stand righteous in the judgment.
5. Pray for the members of your Bible study group.

VI. Some Reflections

1. Memorize Psalm 1 from your favorite translation.
2. Look at a sturdy tree—think how it typifies your obedient life to God.
3. Read Psalm 19, the study for next time.

2 The Glory of God's Work and Word

PSALM 19

Our Milky Way is only one of billions of celestial systems. Each includes stars, nebulae, star clusters, globular clusters, and interstellar matter that make up the universe. No wonder the Psalmist sang, "The heavens declare the glory of God" (19:1).

This psalm is titled, "To the chief Musician, A Psalm of David" (KJV). It is one of the most profound and comprehensive. Here is a wisdom psalm in which David relates the glory of God's work to the perfection and power of His Word.

The theme of the psalm is the sure revelation of God. Tied to His revelation through creation, and in His Word, we see also God's revelation in personal experience. When God thus reveals His works and His will, we are moved to personal response.

Graham Scroggie notes a progress of doctrine. God is first revealed in nature (vv. 1-6), then in Scripture (vv. 7-11), and finally in experience (vv. 12-14).

Outline
I. God Revealed as Creator (19:1-6)
II. God Reveals His Will Through His Word (19:7-11)
III. God's Word Enters Man's Experience (19:12-14)

Joseph Addison wrote a hymn paraphrasing this scriptural account of God's work. Read aloud in unison the following stanzas.

The Heavens Declare His Glory

The spacious firmament on high,
With all the blue ethereal sky,
And spangled heavens, a shining frame,
Their great Original proclaim:

The unwearied sun, from day to day,
Does his Creator's power display,
And publishes to every land
The work of an almighty hand.

What though in solemn silence all
Move round the dark terrestrial ball?
What though no real voice nor sound
Amid the radiant orbs be found?
In reason's ear they all rejoice,
And utter forth a glorious voice;
Forever singing as they shine,
"The hand that made us is divine."

Begin the session with several prayers praising God for the wonder of His creation. Ask for three volunteers to read the three portions of Psalm 19 aloud from the NIV: verses 1-6, the revelation of the heavens; verses 7-11, the law is celebrated; verses 12-14, man's response.

I. God Revealed as Creator (Read 19:1-6)

Philosopher Immanuel Kant once said, "There are two things of perennial wonder, the starry sky and the moral law."

David, from his earliest days, studied from both sources. I can imagine that he wrote this psalm in the first flush of sunrise, when the sun was "like a bridegroom coming forth from his pavilion" (v. 5).

A. Nature Bears Witness to God

John Wesley said the heavens are as legible as a book, but the heathen confuse the issue; they worship the heavenly bodies as gods.

1. Should we attempt to prove the existence of God from nature? Yes _____ No _____ Why? _____

2. The heavens do not tell of God's will, grace, mercy, or love. But they do declare four other elements of His divine being. Supply the appropriate word:

v. 1 _____ v. 2 _____
v. 1 _____ v. 6 _____

3. How would you define God's glory? _____

B. The Plural Glory of the Heavens

Charles Spurgeon speaks of the watery heavens with their clouds of

2 / THE GLORY OF GOD'S WORK AND WORD

countless forms; the aerial heavens with their calms and tempests; the solar heavens with all the glories of the day; and the starry heavens with all the marvels of the night.

1. Circle the following statements true or false.
   T F All things in nature tell the glory of God.
   T F The firmament is the space occupied by the stars and planets.
   T F The heavenly bodies show forth the glory of God by their number, variety, brightness, beauty, and movement.
2. Where in verses 1-6 do you see references to:
   a. God's wisdom—v. _____
   b. His power—v. _____
   c. His supreme knowledge—v. _____
   d. His universal presence—v. _____
   e. His self-revelation—v. _____

C. The Truth by the Creator

The universe supplies a wordless but eloquent witness to the nature of God.

1. What do you think verse 3 means? _____

2. What verse (or verses) show the universality of the proclamation of God's glory? (Read Rom. 10:18.) _____

D. A Symbol of God's Blessings (vv. 4-6)

1. List some figurative words used with regard to the sun's activity.
   a. _____
   b. _____
   c. _____

2. Jesus said the sun is made to shine "on the evil and the good" (Matt. 5:45). What does this teach us about God? _____

II. God Reveals His Will Through His Word (Read 19:7-11)

The glorious revelation of nature must be supplemented by God's revealed Word. "The law of the Lord" (v. 7) is the specific subject of this section. Remember that "law" *(torah)* means not only the commandments; it includes the total teaching of God's revealed will throughout Scripture.

A. God's Law Is Declared

1. List eight statements made.

v. 7a—
v. 7b—
v. 8a—
v. 8b—
v. 9a—
v. 9b—
v. 10—
v. 11—

2. The spiritual teaching of the law (vv. 7-9) is described by six titles, six attributes, and six effects. Fill in the blanks.

Titles	Attributes	Effects
a. Law	Perfect	Restores the soul
b. _____	Trustworthy	_____
c. _____	_____	Joy to the heart
d. Commands	_____	_____
e. _____	Pure	_____
f. Ordinances	_____	_____

3. What do you think the Psalmist meant by the following words?
   a. Perfect—_____
   b. Trustworthy—_____
   c. Right—_____
   d. Radiant—_____
   e. Pure—_____
   f. Sure—_____

4. Discuss in your group what it means to "fear" the Lord.
   a. To be afraid of Him? Yes ____ No ____
   b. To reverence Him? Yes ____ No ____
   c. To obey Him? Yes ____ No ____

B. The Value and Effect of the Law (vv. 10-11)

Read in unison Jas. 1:22-25. What response to the law of God does James see as most important? _____

1. In the space below write the portions of verses 9-10 that fit the following statements:
   a. There are riches in possessing the law. _____
   b. Those who seek the law find pleasure in it. _____

2 / THE GLORY OF GOD'S WORK AND WORD

  c. There is protection for those who observe the law. _____

  d. There is profit to those who obey the law. _____

 2. Share with the group some blessing that has come to your life as a result of following God's will.

III. God's Word Enters Man's Experience (Read 19:12-14)

The greater our knowledge of God's will, the clearer is our view of wrongdoing. The Psalmist declares that only God's grace can cleanse and keep us from sin.

A. David's Prayer

 1. List five results of what following God's will means in life.

  v. 12a _____

  v. 12b _____

  v. 13a _____

  v. 13b _____

  v. 14 _____

 2. Make David's prayer your own, by repeating verses 12-14 in your prayer time each day this week.

B. A Quickened Conscience (vv. 12-13)

The law reveals both the holy character of God and the depravity of the human heart.

 1. God holds us responsible for what we know. But are we also accountable for what we might have known? Yes _____ No _____ Why? _____

 2. Share with the group some way God has revealed His will to you: Bible reading, prayer, sermon, life situation, or other experiences.

C. A Confident Heart (v. 14)

 1. What does the Psalmist see as the basis of his assurance before God? _____

 2. When may we believe our prayers will be heard? _____

IV. Afterglow

1. Reflect on who God is—and believe, wonder, and worship.

2. Read the whole psalm aloud in unison. Observe again how its three portions progress in thought.

3. There is no contradiction between divine revelation and science. Nature, Scripture, and man are but three parts of God's story. The divine creative word preceded the written Word, and both reveal the Incarnate Word, Jesus Christ.

V. Prayer Time

When you pray:

1. Thank God for His revealed truth in nature.
2. Praise Him for the faithfulness of His Word, the Bible.
3. Ask God to apply His Word to you, meeting a present problem.
4. Seek to ever be acceptable in God's sight.

VI. Some Reflections

1. Memorize Ps. 19:12-14 from your favorite translation.

2. Read Psalm 22. It is the first in a trilogy of poems that we study during our next three sessions.

3 The Sob and the Song

PSALM 22

Crying and singing are usually not companions. But hope can change the sob to a song.

Psalm 22 is the first of a moving trilogy of David's psalms, together with 23 and 24. They have been captioned "The Savior," "The Shepherd," and "The Sovereign"; also "The Cross," "The Crook," and "The Crown" (BBC, 3:188).

Psalm 22 is classified as Messianic. It was understood of the Messiah by the Hebrew doctors, by Christ himself, and by His apostles. Christians have long noted the portions that describe Christ's experiences, because the New Testament quotes the psalm seven times in relation to Jesus. Verse 1 appears in Matt. 27:46 and in Mark 15:34; verse 18 is quoted in all four Gospels; and verse 22 appears in Heb. 2:12.

Though other psalms often refer to the kingly nature of the Messiah's office, Psalms 22 and 69 join Isaiah 53 in showing the suffering Messiah. Thus the Old Testament foresees both the crown and the Cross for the coming Deliverer. Popular Jewish thought, however, obscured the Cross behind the crown. Emphasis on Messiah's glorious political reign obscured the redemptive ministry He must have.

In this psalm David is viewed as a type of Christ. While many passages of the psalm may be literally understood of David, some have also a deeper reference to Christ himself.

The psalm has two distinct movements. The first (vv. 1-21) voices a theme of suffering. The second (vv. 22-31) bursts into joyful praise. The key to part one is "O my God, . . . you do not answer" (v. 2). The key to part two is "He . . . has listened to his cry for help" (v. 24). The first records the victim's humiliation; the second, the victor's exaltation.

Outline
I. The Humiliation (22:1-21)
II. The Exaltation (22:22-31)

Choose three people to read aloud each of the three following sections from their favorite version of the Bible. Note the outline of each section as it is read.

A Survey Reading

The first, "Why are you so far from saving me . . . ?" covers verses 1-10. This passage includes: *(a)* a cry of distress (vv. 1-2); *(b)* an expression of confidence (vv. 3-5); *(c)* a description of foes (vv. 6-8); *(d)* a second statement of confidence (vv. 9-10).

The second poetical section, "Do not be far from me," includes verses 11-18. It gives two descriptions: *(a)* surrounding enemies (vv. 11-13); and *(b)* the sufferer's experiences (vv. 14-18).

The third section, "O Lord, be not far off," covers verses 19-31. The tone anticipates salvation and victory (vv. 19-21); testifies in praise (vv. 22-26); and foretells resurrection life (vv. 27-31) (*Christian Workers Commentary*, p. 221).

I. The Humiliation (Read 22:1-21)

The immediate question is: Who is the sufferer? The cry uttered by the Psalmist in verse 1 rings in agony from the parched lips of the crucified Savior 1,000 years later. In some respects, David here describes the sufferings of Jesus Christ on the Cross more vividly than the writers of the Gospels. But we believe every passage in the Old Testament was written first with meaning for those who were then involved.

A. David as Victim

It was the Psalmist himself whose faith was tried by despair, and he cried to God amidst his forsakenness.

1. Have you experienced the seeming hidings of God amid life's turmoil? Yes ____ No ____ Discuss with the group how you felt.

2. List at least five verses from this section (vv. 1-21) that press claims of faith despite God's silence.

  a. _____ d. _____

  b. _____ e. _____

  c. _____

3. From verse 3, what characteristic of God does David grasp as support for his faith? _____

4. How would you define God's holiness? _____

5. Write out three verses that speak of pressure and humiliation.

3 / THE SOB AND THE SONG

a.

b.

c.

6. Circle the statements true or false.
    T F Holiness refers to God's righteousness—His goodness.
    T F A righteous God must reward good and punish evil.
    T F Psalm 1 describes the holiness of God.
7. In verses 4-5, what does the Psalmist use as grounds for his faith?

    a. _____

    b. In verses 9-10? _____

8. What experiences of persecution can you recall from David's life that might have been the occasion for this psalm?

    a. _____

    b. _____

9. Discuss in the group some lessons you think David may have learned from suffering. What does this passage teach us about our responses to suffering? _____

B. Christ as Victim

Have someone read aloud Matt. 27:46. Jesus' cry from the Cross quotes verse 1a. He was utterly forsaken by God as He bore our sins. Read aloud in unison verses 14-18 which graphically describe the horrors of crucifixion. Now invite someone to read for the group Matt. 27:27-36, 41-46.

1. Note the parallels in Psalm 22: Jesus' dying cry (v. 1); mockers taunting Him around the Cross (vv. 6-7, 12-13); parched tongue and lips (v. 15); the act of crucifixion (v. 16); the divided garments and untorn vesture (v. 18).

2. Does the crucifixion of Jesus seem to fulfill this account of tragic suffering? Yes ____ No ____ Why? _____

3. Our Lord's suffering brings us in worship to the foot of His cross. You may want to sing softly together Isaac Watts' familiar hymn:

> *Alas! and did my Savior bleed,*
> *And did my Sov'reign die?*
> *Would He devote that sacred head*
> *For such a worm as I?*

Was it for crimes that I have done
 He groaned upon the tree?
Amazing pity, grace unknown,
 And love beyond degree!

Well might the sun in darkness hide,
 And shut his glories in
When Christ, the mighty Maker, died
 For man, the creature's, sin.

But drops of grief can ne'er repay
 The debt of love I owe.
Here, Lord, I give myself away;
 'Tis all that I can do!

CHORUS
At the Cross, at the Cross, where I first saw the light,
 And the burden of my heart rolled away,
It was there by faith I received my sight,
 And now I am happy all the day!
 —Chorus by Ralph E. Hudson

II. The Exaltation (Read 22:22-31)

Immediately after reading verse 21, a profound silence seems to occur. It is as though death had won. But in verse 22, a shout of renewed life sounds. The glimmer of hope and trust in God is vindicated, and the flickering flame becomes a beacon of light for the future.

A. David as Victor

According to KJV, and a footnote in NIV, the Psalmist views his deliverance as already accomplished, "For thou hast heard me" (v. 21b).

1. When we trust in God, must we wait for actual deliverance to be sure of it? Yes ____ No ____ Why? _____

2. David's praise resounds as his prayer kindles his faith. He who had sobbed now sings. How many times does the word or the concept of praise occur in verses 22-31? _____

3. Ask a member to read aloud verse 22; then another to read Heb. 2:12. Do you think the "congregation" in verse 22 is the same as "the church" (KJV) in Heb. 2:12? Yes ____ No ____ Why? _____

3 / THE SOB AND THE SONG

4. In worship, the Psalmist appeals to those who fear the Lord to praise Him. What does it mean to fear the Lord? _____

5. Circle the following statements true or false.
   T F David's call to worship grew out of his own experience.
   T F God is both the Source and the Object of His people's praise.
   T F Thanksgiving and offerings help fulfill "my vows" (v. 25).

6. In verse 26, what is the relation between seeking and praising the Lord? Which is cause and which is result? _____

7. As you read verses 27-28, do you think David foresees God's redemption for all mankind? Yes _____ No _____

8. As you read verses 30-31, how do you think our own faith in God relates to others from the past? _____

How does it relate to persons yet unborn? _____

B. Christ as Victor

Scroggie declares that verses 22-31 predict Christ's universal kingdom. "It is a gospel before the Gospels, and an Apocalypse before revelation." Thus the future is redeemingly related to the past (*The Psalter*, 1:74).

At verse 22, the psalm breaks from the Crucifixion theme and speaks of the Resurrection. Also, "I will declare your name to my brothers" is applied to Christ who extends His name to all His disciples (Matt. 12:48-50; Heb. 2:11-12).

1. With the Messianic reign, all the nations of the world will become "the kingdom of our Lord and of his Christ" (cf. v. 28; Rev. 11:15). Do you think these verses speak of time or eternity? Why? _____

2. Where do Christians usually place the Messianic reign in time?

3. What do you think it means to say that Jesus Christ is Lord of history? _____

4. Compare verse 29 with Phil. 2:10, "every knee [shall] bow" before the Lord. Do you think these scriptures refer to the same event? Yes _____ No _____

5. Verses 30-31 tell of the ongoing worship of Christ—people of future generations will hear of His righteousness. What do you think is the meaning of the last clause, "for he has done it" (v. 31)? _____

6. Do you think this clause could refer to Jesus' last word from the Cross, "It is finished" (John 19:30)? Yes _____ No _____

7. Jesus endured the Cross, despised the shame, and was raised from the dead, for your salvation and mine. Can you think of at least three ways believers will be exalted with Christ?

   a. _____

   b. _____

   c. _____

III. Afterglow

1. Reflect on the truth that all believers must sometimes enter the Gethsemane of prayer and take up their cross when God seems to have vanished.

2. Recall how your own faith has grown in times of severe trial. Share with the group any recent victory.

IV. Prayer Time

When you pray:

1. Remember, God hears your cry even when it seems He doesn't.

2. Praise God for His goodness and faithfulness to each member of your group.

3. Pray for personal or family needs represented by your study group.

V. Some Reflections

1. We may ask, God, "Why?" if we trustingly await His answer.

2. Memorize Psalm 23 from your favorite Bible version.

4   The Lord as Shepherd and Host

PSALM 23

Who among us wants to tend a flock of wandering, bleating, and smelly sheep? Too often we romanticize the mundane and overlook life's day-by-day realities. But David found God in his daily tasks.

This psalm and the Lord's Prayer are perhaps the two best-known scripture portions. Being so familiar with "The Shepherd's Psalm," we must not take its truths for granted. Both its literary beauty and spiritual insight are unsurpassed. In its message, people of every age, race, and circumstance have received peace and hope for their troubled hearts.

The psalm has been captioned "The Shepherd." Simple trust in the Lord is its theme. David pictures the trusting heart in loving fellowship with God. He is with his Shepherd and Protector in bright days and in dark days, in joy and in sorrow, in peril and in safety. Throughout, the psalm breathes thanksgiving for the never-failing goodness of the Lord.

David may have composed this poem while only a youthful shepherd, tending his father's flocks. His thoughts were inspired in the same field near Bethlehem where 1,000 years later, angels announced Christ's birth to the shepherds.

The whole psalm may be interpreted as the relationship between Shepherd and sheep. The Lord is the Shepherd and we are the sheep. We rejoice in the possessive, "my shepherd," and depend on Him for the future, "I shall not want" (KJV).

The poem blends contrasted images which depict the major aspects of human life, namely: outdoors (vv. 1-2), indoors (6b), pastoral peace (2), pilgrimage through peril (4), the possibility of evil (4b), the prospect of good (5), times of soul renewal (3a), times of ominous gloom (4a), following the Guide (1-2), and a life of security (6b) (BBC, 3:193).

James M. Gray views the psalm in a helpful manner. When the Lord is your Shepherd, you are:

      Feeding on the Word—"pastures"

Fellowshiping the Spirit—"waters"
Being renewed—"restores"
Surrendered in will—"leads"
Trusting the promises—"fear no evil"
Enjoying security—"a table"
Doing service—"overflows"
Possessing hope—"forever" (CWC, p. 221).

This psalm suggests three scenes:

Outline

I. The Shepherd and the Sheep (23:1-3*a*)
II. The Guide and the Pilgrim (23:3*b*-4)
III. The Host and the Guest (23:5-6)

Scroggie says such a division relates the three great truths of God's provision, direction, and communion.

Repeat Psalm 23 together.

Francis Rous wrote a familiar hymn paraphrase entitled "The Twenty-third Psalm."

> *The Lord's my Shepherd, I'll not want:*
> *He makes me down to lie*
> *In pastures green; he leadeth me*
> *The quiet waters by.*

I. The Shepherd and the Sheep (Read 23:1-3*a*)

Imagine yourself in the Shepherd's field near Bethlehem. The Shepherd is the Lord himself. You and I, along with David, are the sheep. Though a flock is implied, the relationship between Shepherd and sheep is personal. "The Lord is *my* shepherd."

A. The Needs of the Sheep

1. Consider the needs of the sheep for which the Shepherd provides. Circle the statements true or false.

   T F Once I was poor.
   T F Once I was weary.
   T F Once I was hungry.
   T F Once I was thirsty.

2. David reminds us that on our own, we are poor, empty, and lost. Under such circumstances will just any shepherd do? Yes ____ No ____

4 / THE LORD AS SHEPHERD AND HOST

B. The Abundant Provision
1. List four provisions given (vv. 1-3a).
   a. _____ c. _____
   b. _____ d. _____
2. In John 10, Jesus calls himself the Good Shepherd, who gives His life for the sheep. This divine Shepherd watches over those in His care. Circle the personal salvation statements true or false.
   T F Jesus is all I need.
   T F Jesus satisfies my longings.
   T F Jesus always leads me in safe paths (v. 5).
   T F Jesus is with me to sustain me day by day.
3. Compare stanza two of Rous's hymn with Ps. 23:3.

   > *My soul he doth restore again;*
   > *And me to walk doth make*
   > *Within the paths of righteousness,*
   > *E'en for his own name's sake.*

II. The Guide and the Pilgrim (Read 23:3b-4)

The scene changes from the pasture to the pathway of life. Throughout all our lives, the Lord guides us. He gives us personal attention though many throng the way.

A. Plight of the Pilgrim
1. Consider the pilgrim:
   a. One becomes lost, going his own way: Yes ____ No ____
   b. The peril of hardships and trials beset all people: Yes ____ No ____
   c. Death is a dark passage all must go through: Yes ____ No ____
   d. Evil seems ever-present: Yes ____ No ____
2. Does David imply the pilgrim needs a guide as badly as a sheep needs a faithful shepherd? Yes ____ No ____
3. What do you think it means to "fear no evil"? _____
_____
4. Why do you think death is spoken of as a "shadow" and not utter darkness? _____
5. Discuss with the group how you feel about death. Will the presence of the Lord be as real after physical death as during this life? Yes ____ No ____ Why? _____

B. The Faithful Guide

1. Affirm together the character of the guide. Read in unison this declaration of faith.

I believe God guides in paths of righteousness.
I have found He supplies courage when the way is threatening.
I am sure He knows the path I take.
I know that He is with me in life and will go with me through the valley of death.

2. Why do you think David believed the Lord knew where to lead him? _____

3. Can you recall some occasion when God helped you make a difficult decision? If so, be prepared to share the experience with your group.

4. Ask a member to read aloud Ps. 23:4.
Read in unison this third stanza of Rous's hymn:

> Yea, though I walk through death's dark vale,
> Yet will I fear no ill;
> For thou art with me, and thy rod
> And staff me comfort still.

5. To what do you think David referred by the shepherd's "rod" and "staff"?

    a. Rod—_____
    b. Staff—_____

How did they "comfort" the sheep? _____

There are seven sufficiencies of the Shepherd (23:1-4):
    a. "I shall not want for complete satisfaction" (v. 1a).
    b. "I shall not want for guidance" (v. 2b).
    c. "I shall not want for renewal" (v. 3a).
    d. "I shall not want for instruction in righteousness" (v. 3b).
    e. "I shall not want for courage in danger" (v. 4a).
    f. "I shall not want for the Divine Presence" (v. 4b).
    g. "I shall not want for comfort in sorrow" (v. 4c). (BBC, 3:194-95)

6. Be prepared to share with the group how you have found the Lord to be your Shepherd in one of the above experiences.

III. The Host and the Guest (Read 23:5-6)

This passage depicts the safety of home. David names the Lord as Host and himself as the guest.

4 / THE LORD AS SHEPHERD AND HOST

A. The Personal Needs of the Guest
1. List four ways the Host provides for the guest. Fill in the blanks.
   a. A table _____
   b. His head _____
   c. His cup _____
   d. Abiding place _____

2. Which of the above provisions seems most meaningful to your own experience? _____

B. The Provision by the Host
1. Discuss four positive results.
   a. My enemies are kept from injuring me.
   b. He supplies my physical needs.
   c. Goodness and mercy (loving-kindness) support my spirit.
   d. He promises a place in the house of the Lord forever.

2. The Hebrew word for mercy *(chesed)* means covenant love, grace. Why do you think David could be so confident of the Lord's loving-kindness? _____
_____

3. What covenant assures us of God's goodness and mercy? _____
_____

4. What do you think "I will dwell in the house of the Lord forever" meant to David? _____
What does it mean to you? _____
Invite a member to read aloud the last two verses of Rous's hymn:

> *A table thou hast furnished me*
> *In presence of my foes;*
> *My head thou dost with oil anoint,*
> *And my cup overflows.*
>
> *Goodness and mercy all my life*
> *Shall surely follow me;*
> *And in God's house for evermore*
> *My dwelling place shall be.*

C. The Name Jehovah (Lord) Fully Defined
The Old Testament uses the name Jehovah with a descriptive suffix seven times. All seven are found in this psalm.
1. Jehovah-Rohi, the Lord my Shepherd (v. 1).
2. Jehovah-Shalom, the Lord my Peace (v. 2; Judg. 6:24).

3. Jehovah-Ropheca, the Lord my Health (v. 3; Exod. 15:26).
4. Jehovah-Tsidkenu, the Lord my Righteousness (v. 3; Jer. 23:6).
5. Jehovah-Shammah, the Lord my Companion (v. 4; Ezek. 48:35).
6. Jehovah-Nissi, the Lord my Victory (v. 5; Exod. 17:15).
7. Jehovah-Jireh, the Lord my Provision (v. 6; Gen. 22:14).

IV. Afterglow

1. The same Lord is over all—available to all. This psalm has inspired millions to live and die trusting the ever-present Lord.

2. How has Psalm 23 enriched your personal devotion to God?

3. Hope for the future stems from present abiding with God.

V. Prayer Time

When you pray:
1. Thank God for His tender care during unknown danger.
2. Praise Him for food, clothing, and shelter.
3. Ask the Lord to keep you from the snares of evil.
4. Confess your total dependence on His guidance to gain life eternal.

VI. Some Reflections

1. Jesus affirms the truth of this psalm. Read John 14:1-3.
2. The Good Shepherd is with me in life or in death.
3. For next week read the third psalm of this trilogy—Psalm 24.

5 Worship the King of Glory

PSALM 24

Whom—or what—shall we worship? Someone or something will receive our wholehearted commitment.

The third psalm of David's trilogy is a poem of worship. It may have been written when the ark of the Lord was brought from the house of Obed-edom to the Tabernacle on Mount Zion (2 Sam. 6:1-15). David here seems to envision the Temple he yearned to build.

This psalm has been called "The Sovereign" and "The Crown." The message is often interpreted as prophetic of Christ's ascension. It marks His victory over sin and death (v. 8) and His future sovereignty over all (v. 10).

The poem was used in Israel's worship in various ways. Perhaps the singing began at the foot of the hill on which Jerusalem stood. One choir of worshipers sang verses 1-3, a second sang verses 4-6. In front of the city gates, the first choir sang verse 7; the second responded with verse 8a. The first choir chanted verses 8b and 9; the second choir asked the question in verse 10a, and the first choir replied with verse 10b.

Graham Scroggie says certain psalms were sung in morning worship at the Temple each day of the week. On Saturday, the Sabbath, it was Psalm 92; on Sunday, Psalm 24; Monday, Psalm 48; Tuesday, Psalm 82; Wednesday, Psalm 94; Thursday, Psalm 81; and on Friday, Psalm 93 (*The Psalter*, 1:81).

John Wesley divides Psalm 24 into three portions: (1) God's sovereignty over the world (vv. 1-2); (2) Who shall receive His blessing (vv. 3-6); (3) An exhortation to receive Christ (vv. 7-10).

Outline

The psalm divides itself into two major sections.
    I. True Worship (24:1-6)
    II. Coronation of the King (24:7-10)

Divide your group into two choirs, and read Psalm 24 responsively.

First choir: vv. 1-3
Second choir: vv. 4-6
First choir: v. 7
Second choir: v. 8a
First choir: vv. 8b-9
Second choir: v. 10a
First choir: v. 10b

How many concepts from Psalm 24 occur in this hymn written by Charles Wesley? _____

The King of Glory

Our Lord is risen from the dead;
  Our Jesus is gone up on high;
The powers of hell are captive led,
  Dragged to the portals of the sky:
There his triumphal chariot waits,
  And angels chant the solemn lay:
"Lift up your heads, ye heavenly gates;
  Ye everlasting doors, give way!

"Loose all your bars of massy light,
  And wide unfold the ethereal scene;
He claims these mansions as his right;
  Receive the King of glory in!"
"Who is the King of glory? Who?"
  "The Lord, that all our foes o'ercame;
The world, sin, death, and hell o'er threw;
  And Jesus is the Conqueror's name."

I. True Worship (Read 24:1-6)

The Almighty One of Israel is declared to be the universal Sovereign. The psalm exalts God as the Creator of all mankind, and glories in His acts to save His chosen people.

A. The Lord Worshiped (vv. 1-2)

1. Why do you think no limits are placed upon God's authority and dominion? _____

2. Besides being the Creator of all things, the New Testament adds a further reason to worship God. Read 1 Pet. 1:18-19. What is that reason?

_____

3. What two facts made David think the Lord was worthy of all worship?

5 / WORSHIP THE KING OF GLORY

v. 1 _____

v. 2 _____

4. Does the character of the God who is worshiped mold the character of the worshipers? Yes _____ No _____

B. Holy Worshipers Required (vv. 3-6)

The Almighty has revealed himself to us as the Holy God. Thus His people must be holy. Read Ps. 15:1-5 and Isa. 33:14-17.

1. Verse 3 asks a question in poetic parallelism: "Who may ascend the hill of the Lord? Who may stand in his holy place?" Verse 4 gives the answer. Write it below. _____

2. List the four requirements of worship found in verse 4.

   a. (An outward expression)—_____

   b. (An inward condition)—_____

   c. (An inward condition)—_____

   d. (An outward expression)—_____

3. What does "clean hands" mean? _____

4. Read Zech. 13:1. The prophet foretells a fountain opened to the house of David for sin and uncleanness. If hands refer to what one does, what does a "pure heart" mean? _____

5. How is one's soul lifted up to an idol? (Read 1 John 2:15-17.)

6. Circle the following statements true or false.

   T F Forgiveness of sins and cleansing from inner pollution are required to stand in God's presence (Ps. 51:7-10; Jas. 4:8).

   T F Idols are false gods.

   T F Worship of idols is sinful because they take the place of God.

   T F We can deceive others and ourselves, but not God.

7. Verse 5 declares the heritage of holy worshipers. In what ways are they vindicated? _____

8. Verse 6 implies that true children of God seek Him. They seek His face. What do you think it means to seek the face of God? _____

9. John Wesley says God's grace and favor is often called God's face. Does this seem like a helpful explanation? Yes _____ No _____

Selah (v. 6) means "Pause and meditate."

II. Coronation of the King (Read 24:7-10)

We envision the ascending company of worshipers pausing as they reach the city gates. They stand before the temporary Tabernacle. By faith and the spirit of prophecy, the gates and doors of the Temple are spoken of as already built.

A. The Call—"Lift up your heads, O you gates" (v. 7)

The gates are personified and called upon to open with dignity and reverence so that the "King of glory" might enter.

1. Do you think this passage has a personal application, opening our lives to Christ? Yes _____ No _____ Why? _____

_____

2. Why do you think these gates are spoken of as "ancient doors"?

_____

3. John Wesley viewed the Temple as a type of Christ and of heaven itself. Do you agree? Yes _____ No _____ Why? _____

_____

4. Might this passage refer to Christ's ascension into heaven, where the saints and angels are mentioned as preparing the way for their Lord and King? Yes _____ No _____

    5. Circle the statements true or false.

        T F The King of glory is One to whom all glory should be ascribed.

        T F The King of glory is the Messiah.

        T F The King of glory is the king of Israel.

B. The Challenge (vv. 8-10)

The first challenge is: "Who is this King of glory?" The answer is: "The Lord strong and mighty, the Lord mighty in battle" (v. 8).

    1. Circle the following statements true or false.

        T F The Lord is Jehovah God.

        T F The Lord proves His might by subduing every foe.

    2. Verse 9 repeats the call of verse 7; verse 10 again answers, "The Lord Almighty" (NIV); "The Lord of hosts" (KJV, NASB)—"he is the King of glory." In what ways do you perceive God as King?

        a. _____

        b. _____

    3. Circle the statements true or false.

5 / WORSHIP THE KING OF GLORY

      T F God is Captain both of the armies of Israel and of the hosts of heaven.

      T F The terms "the Lord Almighty" and "the Lord of hosts" cannot refer to King David.

III. Afterglow

1. Notice some contrasts in this coronation poem:
    a. The earthly king and the heavenly King.
    b. The physical setting and spiritual worship.
    c. The present and the future.
2. Jesus Christ will be crowned King of Kings in the new Jerusalem.

IV. Prayer Time

When you pray:

1. Begin with self-examination, desiring clean hands and a pure heart.
2. Thank God for the beauty of His creation.
3. Praise God that His salvation plan includes you.
4. Repeat the Lord's Prayer together.

V. Some Reflections

1. Jesus fulfills the ancient role as Savior, Shepherd, and King.
2. Is Jesus Christ King of my life?
3. Read Psalm 37 in preparation for the next lesson.

6   Don't Worry—Trust God

PSALM 37

There is no profit in worry. But great comfort and gain come to those who trust God.

Psalm 37, titled "A Psalm of David," is a wisdom psalm. It is one of three, together with 49 and 73, dealing with the nagging problem of the prosperity of the wicked.

The material success of the wicked and the adversity of the righteous has always been hard to resolve, especially for the ancients. The Old Testament gave no clear revelation of final judgment when everyone receives just reward or punishment for his deeds. Scroggie suggests we should consider two other facts also. First, material wealth was viewed as the token of God's blessing, and poverty was considered a divine punishment. It was also believed that "the law of retribution and recompense could be traced in the destinies of the family if not of the individual" (*The Psalter*, 1:126).

The Psalmist finds help when God reminds him that the success of the wicked is only temporary. David's opening injunction, "Do not fret" (NIV), "Fret not" (KJV), is the key to the psalm.

This is an acrostic psalm. Each successive letter of the Hebrew alphabet begins alternate lines. Generally, two lines are under each letter. Most of the pairs of verses are complete and self-contained, much like individual proverbs.

Outline

A fully satisfactory outline is elusive, but four major sections may be noted and described.

    I. Exhortations to Commitment (37:1-11)
   II. Catastrophe Awaits the Wicked (37:12-22)
  III. Confidence of the Righteous (37:23-31)
  IV. Contrast Between the Righteous and the Wicked (37:32-40)

6 / DON'T WORRY—TRUST GOD

Read Psalm 37 aloud, each person of the group reading two verses, except those who read the single verses, 7, 20, 29, and 34. This reading will mark the alphabetical acrostic feature of the psalm.

Note how this hymn translated by John Wesley refers to Psalm 37.

Whoso Putteth His Trust in the Lord

Commit thou all thy griefs
And ways into his hands,
To his sure trust and tender care
Who earth and heaven commands.

Thou on the Lord rely,
So, safe, shalt thou go on;
Fix on his work thy steadfast eye,
So shall thy work be done.

Thy everlasting truth,
Father, thy ceaseless love,
Sees all thy children's wants, and knows
What best for each will prove.

—Paul Berhardt

I. Exhortations to Commitment (Read 37:1-11)

David faces the questions of the righteous who face the inequities of life. He testifies that one's commitment to God brings contentment despite the contradictions of experience.

A. Duties Enjoined on the Godly Person (vv. 1, 3-8)

1. List four duties found in verses 1, 7-8.
    a. _____ c. _____
    b. _____ d. _____
2. Circle the following statements true or false.
    T F To cease from doing wrong, one must forsake it.
    T F We should seek to solve moral mysteries. Explain your answer. _____
3. List six positive exhortations found in verses 3-5, 7.
    a. _____ d. _____
    b. _____ e. _____
    c. _____ f. _____
4. Circle the following statements true or false.

T F God's exhortations may be summarized by the words "faith" and "patience."
T F Both time and trust are factors in God's government of the world.
T F We should use time doing good rather than waste it worrying over others doing evil.

B. Why Commitment Is Urged (vv. 2, 9-11)

V. 2. The triumph of the wicked is (1) short-lived _____ (2) permanent _____.

Vv. 9-11. Those who hope in the Lord (1) are better off now _____ (2) will finally come out best _____.

How firm is my faith that verses 9-11 are true? (1) I don't really believe it. _____ (2) I hope it is true. _____ (3) I am staking my whole future on this truth. _____ Circle the following statements true or false.

T F The disparities of life are forever.
T F The meek shall inherit the earth and live in peace.
T F Evil's success is only apparent; the failure of the godly is only seeming.

II. Catastrophe Awaits the Wicked (Read 37:12-22)

All but two verses of this section (18-19) describe the disasters awaiting evil men. The Psalmist develops the brevity of life in verses 2, 9-10, to support the believer's faith and patience.

A. Plight of the Wicked (vv. 12-17)

1. Show how the Psalmist expects the scales of justice to be balanced.

Wicked	Righteous
v. 12 Plot and rage	v. 13 _____
v. 14 Draw the sword	v. 15 _____
v. 16 Ill-gotten wealth	v. 17 _____

2. Circle the following statements true or false.
   T F God sees the future as well as the present.
   T F Evil returns like a boomerang upon the heads of evildoers.
   T F The value of poverty and riches are determined by their effect upon character.

B. Life's Final Outcome (vv. 18-22)

1. List some ways the Lord shows He knows the righteous.

6 / DON'T WORRY—TRUST GOD

    v. 18 _____
    v. 19 _____
    v. 19 _____
    v. 22 _____

2. List some perils of the wicked.
    v. 20 _____
    v. 20 _____
    v. 20 _____
    v. 22 _____

III. Confidence of the Righteous (Read 37:23-31)

This section presents the assurance of the righteous. The wicked are mentioned only once—in verse 28.

A. The Lord Orders the Steps of the Righteous (v. 23, KJV)

1. George Muller once said, "The Lord orders the steps, and also the stops of a good man"—the providences that put one on the shelf for a time. Do you agree? If so, why? _____

2. Moffatt translates verse 24, "He may fall, but he never falls down, for the Eternal holds him by the hand." Have you so experienced God's help? Yes ____ No ____ If so, be ready to share your testimony with the group.

B. The Psalmist Testifies (vv. 25-28)

1. In what ways do you think the children of the righteous are blessed?
    a. _____
    b. _____
    c. _____

2. Discuss the impact righteous parents have upon their children's lives. Be ready to share two thoughts with the group.
    a. _____
    b. _____

C. The Secret of Security (vv. 29-31)

1. Circle the following statements true or false.
    T F A righteous life enjoys God's keeping care always.
    T F Uprightness of heart is expressed in one's thought and walk.
    T F Slipping feet indicate a heart straying from God's law.

2. Is our confidence in God (1) conditional _____ (2) unconditional _____? Why do you think so? Discuss with the group.

IV. The Righteous and the Wicked Contrasted (37:32-40)

Here the whole psalm is summarized, contrasting the lots of the righteous and the wicked. The wicked often seem to succeed. The righteous often endure trouble. But the end of the wicked is destruction, while the righteous find a life of peace.

A. The Wicked Oppose the Righteous (vv. 32-33)
1. Circle the following statements true or false.

    T F Those who oppose the righteous also fight against God.

    T F The righteous are helpless against the power of the wicked.

    T F The Lord finally overrules the course of evil men.

B. Contrasting Outcomes of Life (vv. 34-38)
1. Do you think for the righteous there is more good or evil in this life? (1) more evil _____ (2) more good _____

2. Why do you think evil appears to predominate at times? _____

3. David foresees the inheritance of the righteous and the passing power of the wicked. Show the contrast by filling the blanks.

The Righteous	The Wicked
v. 34 _____	v. 34 _____
v. 37 _____	v. 36 _____
	v. 38 _____

C. The Lord Is for the Righteous (vv. 39-40)
1. Circle the statements true or false.

    T F One's well-being comes only by his well-doing.

    T F We escape the wicked by taking refuge in the Lord.

    T F The Lord delivers the righteous and destroys the wicked.

2. List at least two ways the Lord has helped you.

    a. _____

    b. _____

V. Afterglow
1. Premature judgments dishonor God. His help is worth waiting for.

2. Recall the last time you were perplexed with the success of the wicked and the struggles of the righteous. Discuss with the group.

3. It is easier for Christians now to believe in the vindication of the righteous because of Christ's triumph over sin and death.

VI. Prayer Time

When you pray:

1. Declare yourself to be on the Lord's side.

2. Commit your life to His care.

3. Wait patiently before the Lord, seeking His guidance.

4. Praise God for the promise of an eternal inheritance.

5. Share personal needs and prayer requests with one another. Present those concerns to the Lord.

VII. Some Reflections

1. See how the following verses are reinforced by New Testament revelation:
    Ps. 37:4—John 15:7
    Ps. 37:11—Matt. 5:5
    Ps. 37:19—Phil. 4:19
    Ps. 37:21—Acts 20:35
    Ps. 37:31—Heb. 10:16
    Ps. 37:37-38—Rom. 6:23

2. Write out several verses that helped you most. Commit them to memory.

3. Read Psalms 42 and 43 in preparation for the next lesson.

7 The Soul's Thirst for God

PSALMS 42 and 43

Inner longings move us to seek God in His house, or to call upon Him wherever we are.

Chapters 42—72 comprise Book II of the Psalms. They are called "Psalms of the Temple." Of the 31 chapters only 18 are attributed to David. Book II is part of what is known as the "Elohistic psalter," because the name used for the Deity is *Elohim*, "God," rather than *Yahweh*, "the Lord."

Scholars believe Psalms 42 and 43 were originally one poem because Psalm 43 is the only psalm in Book II without a title. Psalm 42 is titled, "To the chief Musician." It is "for the sons of Korah," mentioned in 1 Chron. 9:19 as a guild of Temple servants. Heman, one of the Korahites, was the ancestor of the Temple singers organized by David (1 Chron. 6:31-33). The psalm is also described as "Maschil," which suggests, "to instruct, to make . . . intelligent" (BBC, 3:239).

These two psalms express conflicting emotions which people of God have experienced in all ages. Sorrow and song, doubt and faith, fear and devotion are strangely intermingled.

Psalm 42 is the lament of an exile from the house of God. He sings a sad song among enemies who ridicule his religious convictions. There is a cry for the God whom he knows, and he grieves over his foes mocking God. He longs to be with the worshiping multitudes, both as leader and companion, in God's Temple.

Poetry which depends upon rhyming sound loses its character when translated. Bible poetry, however, can be translated into any language without serious loss because the rhythm of Hebrew poetry is in the recurrence of thought.

Outline
I. Separation (42:1-5)
II. Condemnation (42:6-11)
III. Restoration (43:1-5)

7 / THE SOUL'S THIRST FOR GOD

The three sections of Psalms 42—43 each close with the same refrain: "Why are you downcast, O my soul?" Read Psalms 42 and 43 aloud, verse by verse going around the group. The leader may read the refrain each time, 42:5, 11, and 43:5. Despair and hope are here in tension.

Compare the heart attitudes expressed in these psalms with the ideas in this hymn from Wesley's period:

Faint, Yet Pursuing

As pants the hart for cooling streams,
  When heated in the chase,
So longs my soul, O God, for thee,
  And thy refreshing grace.

For thee, my God, the living God,
  My thirsty soul doth pine;
O when shall I behold thy face,
  Thou Majesty divine?

Why restless, why cast down, my soul?
  Hope still, and thou shalt sing
The praise of him who is thy God,
  Thy Saviour, and thy King.

—Nahum Tate and
Rev. Nicholas Brady

I. Separation (Read 42:1-5)

A. Thirst for Communion with God (vv. 1-2)

The poet compares his longing for God with the thirst of a deer for a cool drink from a mountain stream. Such craving anticipates the beatitude of Jesus, "Blessed are those who hunger and thirst for righteousness, for they will be filled" (Matt. 5:6).

The phrase "the living God" appears here for the first time, revealing the Old Testament concept of the true God. A contrast is drawn with idols which were empty beings, dead in every sense of the word.

No one who truly thirsts for God fails to find Him.

1. Have you ever been kept away from God's house for a long period by illness or isolation? If so, describe your feelings. _____

_____

2. Why do you think fellowship with God in His sanctuary is special?

a. _____
b. _____

3. Circle the following statements true or false.
   T F Cravings for communion with God are only for super-saints.
   T F Hunger and thirst for God is a sign of weakness.
   T F One begins fellowship with God when he earnestly seeks Him.
   T F God will meet us only in His sanctuary.

B. Where Is God? (vv. 3-5)

Sometimes to all appearances God seems to have forsaken us. Like the Psalmist, we become depressed when Satan and his cohorts taunt us with "Where is your God?"

1. Recall some personal experience when God seemed far away. Describe how you felt. _____

2. Why do you think God at times lets us have such experiences? _____

3. Define what the following words mean to you.
   a. Joy—_____
   b. Thanksgiving—_____
   c. Downcast—_____
   d. Disturbed—_____
   e. Hope—_____
   f. Praise—_____

4. A pastor friend has a motto on his study wall: "Praise God Anyhow." What value would such a reminder have? _____

5. Be prepared to share how some period of seeking God has restored you.

II. Condemnation (Read 42:6-11)

The Psalmist again laments the unjust condemnation by his enemies. We are not told why the poet was confined to Mount Mizar, near the peaks of Hermon, east of the Jordan River, but we know that King David fled to this area during the rebellion by his son Absalom.

A. Dealing with Unjust Accusations (vv. 6-10)

The spiritual journey of this troubled seeker included sweeping waves (v. 7), calmed by divine love (v. 8). The sigh of the soul turns to song. When

7 / THE SOUL'S THIRST FOR GOD

we live by faith, mourning awaits God's answer in the morning (vv. 8-9). In hope, we shall yet praise God (v. 11).

  1. Compare the prophet Jonah's experience (Jonah 2:3, 9).
  2. List the phrases asking "Why?" (42:5-11).
     v. 5 _____
     v. 5 _____
     v. 9 _____
     v. 9 _____
     v. 11 _____
     v. 11 _____
  3. Name one or two ways you recognize God as your "Rock."
     a. _____
     b. _____

  4. Have you ever had anyone make fun of you because of your faith in God? Yes _____ No _____ What would be the best answer to the taunt, "Where is your God?" _____

B. A Prayer of Hope (v. 11)

Praising God gave the Psalmist faith that God would restore him.

  1. Give at least two reasons why you think God remembers you.
     a. _____
     b. _____
  2. How important is prayer in quelling feelings of condemnation? Read 1 John 3:19-22. _____
  3. Does prayer help loneliness? Yes _____ No _____ How? _____

III. Restoration (Read 43:1-5)

The theme of hope grows stronger even in the recurring note of lament. Seeking the Divine Presence, the Psalmist calls upon God to vindicate him.

A. A Man Talks to God (vv. 1-3)

  1. The Psalmist put himself into God's hands. Can you recall when you have done this and have found restored assurance? Yes _____ No _____ If so, be prepared to share the experience with your group.
  2. Should we view trials as a sign of being rejected by God? Yes _____ No _____

3. Circle the following statements true or false.
   T F God is faithful in sending His light and truth to guide us.
   T F God leads us to holy living as well as to the place of worship.
   T F God must be our joy and delight before we will praise Him.

B. A Man Speaks to Himself (vv. 4-5)

1. Do we ever have the right to question God? Yes ____ No ____ Why? See verse 2. Someone said that I may ask my questions but I must never doubt God's love, and I must never demand immediate answers.

2. How can I know I am being led in God's way? _____
   a. When the guidance is scriptural: Yes ____ No ____
   b. When it is reasonable: Yes ____ No ____
   c. When the guidance persists as I pray about it: Yes ____ No ____

3. Why is it important that we face up to our own problems? ____

4. How may we stir up our trust in God?
   a. _____
   b. _____

IV. Afterglow

1. God's loving-kindness serves as a lifejacket in a troubled sea.

2. Share with the group how recent hungering and thirsting after God during a trial brought refreshment and growth.

3. God's presence can become so real to us that He wipes away our doubts and fears.

V. Prayer Time

When you pray:
1. Tell God what things trouble you.
2. Ask God to help you hope and trust in Him when He seems silent.
3. Offer yourself to God in special times of worship and service.
4. Allow God's truth to lead you; rest in the joy of His salvation.

VI. Some Reflections

1. The personal God of the Psalms is firm ground for present-day faith to resolve our problems.

2. Divine revelation is not abstract—it comes to us in concrete human experience.

3. Memorize Ps. 43:3.

4. Read 2 Samuel 11—12; also Psalms 32 and 51 in preparation for the next lesson.

8   Plea for Pardon and Purity

PSALM 51

It is never easy to say, "I'm sorry—forgive me!" But it is sometimes necessary.

This is the fourth and best known of the seven Penitential Psalms. The others are Psalms 6; 32; 38; 102; 130; and 143. In Psalm 51 David sought God's mercy after the prophet Nathan accused him of adultery with Bathsheba, and of arranging her husband's death.

The ritual law made no provision for atonement for arrogant sins. But there was forgiveness, even for adultery and murder, when the sinner approached God with a broken spirit and a contrite heart (v. 17). From that humble stance David sought divine pardon.

The melody of this prayer-hymn features five notes. (1) *Sin* is the mournful note (vv. 1-2). (2) There's a serious note of *responsibility*. David's use of personal pronouns shows full and honest confession (vv. 3-5). (3) Throughout is a decisive note of *repentance*. (4) The glad note of *forgiveness* and *cleansing* makes harmony (vv. 7-14). (5) The certain note of *testimony* voices crowning praise (vv. 12-13, 15) (BBC, 3:258).

Even after 3,000 years, these key notes in David's prayer still comprise the sad and joyful music of all mankind. The king's consciousness of sin brought sorrow for it. Every penitent may thus seek God's matchless grace.

Outline

I. Divine Pardon Sought (51:1-4)
II. Man's Sinful Problem Confessed (51:5-9)
III. A New Creation (51:10-13)
IV. Praise and Thanksgiving (51:14-19)

Compare the plea of David with Isaac Watts' hymn of repentance.

8 / PLEA FOR PARDON AND PURITY

Pleading for Pity

Show pity, Lord, O Lord, forgive;
Let a repenting rebel live:
Are not thy mercies large and free?
May not a sinner trust in thee?

O wash my soul from every sin,
And make my guilty conscience clean;
Here on my heart the burden lies,
And past offenses pain my eyes.

Yet save a trembling sinner, Lord,
Whose hope, still hovering round thy word,
Would light on some sweet promise there,
Some sure support against despair.

I. Divine Pardon Sought (Read 51:1-4)

David's remorse made him a qualified seeker after God's grace. His cry arose from a deeply troubled heart rather than a studied religious view. No exact differences are noted between sinful acts and the sinful nature, or between the need for pardon and God's demand for purity. The prayer, however, moves by spiritual insight from the pleas for pardon to the deeper problem of moral cleansing.

A. God's Mercy (vv. 1-2)

1. God's compassion for sinners inspires the cry for forgiveness: Yes ____ No ____

2. "Blot out my transgressions" acknowledges both guilt and expectation of divine intervention. Agree ____ Disagree ____

3. Scroggie defines "transgression" as violation of law; "iniquity" as morally crooked; and "sin" as missing the mark.

B. God's Forgiveness and Cleansing (vv. 3-4)

1. Evildoing is a crime against our fellows, but even more it is sin against God. Yes ____ No ____ Discuss in the group.

2. Circle the following statements true or false.
    T F Only as sin is acknowledged can it be forgiven and cleansed.
    T F David felt God's judgment against sin was too severe.

3. Is remembrance of sin ever for our good? Yes ____ No ____ Why?

4. In what respects do you think David's prayer included the tendency to sin as well as the acts of sin? _____

5. Our evil acts proceed from an evil nature. Yes ____ No ____ Discuss our scriptural responsibility for both evil acts and evil nature.

II. Man's Sinful Problem Confessed (Read 51:5-9)

David traced his filthy life-stream of sin to a corrupt fountain. His conviction deepened to include what he was by nature as well as his sinful deeds. He saw himself a sinner from birth, from the time his mother conceived him.

A. A Sinner from Birth (v. 5)

1. Because man's sinful tendencies and dispositions stem from a racial pollution, the Bible teaches that he is conceived in sin. Agree ____ Disagree ____

2. In his *Explanatory Notes upon the Old Testament* John Wesley interprets David's mood: "I find, that this heinous crime, was the proper fruit of my vile nature, which ever was, and still is ready to commit 10,000 sins, as occasion offers." With this analysis I agree ____ or disagree ____.

3. To what extent do you think every man's problem is the same as David's? _____

B. God's Remedy (vv. 6-9)

1. Circle the statements true or false.

    T F God requires and desires truthfulness in "the inner self" (NBV).

    T F "Whiter than snow" refers to an inner cleansing like pure snowflakes without even a trace of pollution (cf. Isa. 1:18).

    T F Mental anguish such as David's can be transformed to joy and gladness only by God's intervention.

2. God must teach us to know wisdom. Yes ____ No ____ Discuss how God's wisdom is learned.

3. Cleansing, as with hyssop, is both ceremonial and actual. Yes ____ No ____ (Cf. Lev. 14:4; 1 John 1:7.)

4. The pain of crushed bones symbolizes the bitter conviction of sin. Agree ____ Disagree ____

8 / PLEA FOR PARDON AND PURITY

III. A New Creation (Read 51:10-13)

The radical wrong is in our souls—not in our surroundings. David believes divine pardon is possible. As one recognizes and confesses his need, he receives God's restoring work. The results of that purging and washing are a clean heart and the renewal of a steadfast spirit.

A. A Pure Heart and a Steadfast Spirit (vv. 10-11)

1. Circle the following statements true or false.

   T F To create a pure heart means the purging of inward filth, and the restoring a mind and heart made holy by God.

   T F One may have a steadfast spirit without having a pure heart.

   T F A pure heart and a steadfast spirit are the springs of a holy life. They occur only by the creative, life-giving power of God.

2. John Wesley defines spirit as a "disposition of soul." Agree ____ Disagree ____ Discuss your answer with the group.

B. Assurance of God's Presence (vv. 12-13)

1. Divine cleansing assures us of the abiding presence of God's Holy Spirit. Yes ____ No ____

2. Heart purity brings the joy of salvation. Yes ____ No ____

3. How does a "willing spirit" affect the life of one who has been restored? _____

4. To what extent is purity required of those who would teach God's ways to transgressors? (Compare verse 13 with John 16:7-11 and Acts 1:8.)

IV. Praise and Thanksgiving (Read 51:14-19)

The restored feel compelled to tell others what God has wrought in their lives. Praise to God keeps the believer steadfast in faith.

A. Beyond Ritual (vv. 14-17)

1. Ask one member to read aloud verses 16-17. Then invite another to read Ps. 50:7-15. Both passages sound the note of true spiritual repentance. Agree ____ Disagree ____

2. If God is not appeased by sacrifices and burnt offerings, why do you think the sacrificial system was instituted? _____

3. Discuss in the group why a broken spirit and a contrite heart are more effective than religious ritual in conquering sin.

B. General and Personal Obedience (vv. 18-19)

1. How do you think personal righteousness influences national righteousness? _____

2. Discuss the proper relationship between church and state in offering praise and thanksgiving to God.

3. Is God opposed to all ritual? Yes ____ No ____ If not, when is He pleased with it? _____

V. Afterglow

1. Give thanks to God in as loud a voice as sin once had in your life.

2. Can you trace your own Christian pilgrimage parallel to David's pathway, beginning with conviction for sin, and ending with a testimony of praise? Be prepared to share your testimony with one other person in the group.

VI. Prayer Time

When you pray:

1. Confess all your needs to God.
2. Thank God for all His mercies to you.
3. Trust God's pardon and cleansing to bring joy and gladness.
4. Praise God for His redeeming and restoring grace.

VII. Some Reflections

1. Think how the sacrifice of Jesus Christ makes a difference in the content of our prayer for pardon and cleansing.

2. Only God can create a clean heart or a new earth.

3. Read Psalms 49 and 73 in preparation for the next lesson.

9 The Riddle of Life

PSALM 73

When the wicked amass fortunes, whose unseen hand tips the balance scale of life on the side of the righteous?

This is the first of 17 psalms, 73—89, in Book III. All of the titles include personal names. Eleven are ascribed to Asaph; three to Korah; and one each to David, Heman, and Ethan.

This psalm of Asaph is typed as wisdom literature. We have seen that Psalms 1; 19; and 37 are also of this class. Asaph descended from Gershom, son of Levi (1 Chron. 6:39). Fellow Levites chose him as a leading singer when they brought the ark to Jerusalem (1 Chron. 16:4-5). He and David were the authors of the psalms used when King Hezekiah revived the Temple worship (2 Chron. 29:30).

This psalm's language reminds us of Job and the prophet Jeremiah under similar circumstances. The problem is: How can an all-powerful God be good, and still allow the wicked to prosper, while the righteous go unrewarded?

The Psalmist personally wondered whether his faith would survive or succumb. As with Job, it was a life-and-death issue which must be resolved. You and I sometimes face the same problem.

Outline
I. The Problem of the Righteous (73:1-3)
II. The Prosperity of the Wicked (73:4-12)
III. Faith's Struggle (73:13-22)
IV. Faith's Triumph (73:23-28)

Read Psalm 73 aloud, going around the group, using these divisions:
vv. 1-2, Introduction
vv. 3-6, The Wicked Prosper
vv. 7-10, The Calloused Deeds of the Wicked

vv. 11-14, Bold Skeptics
vv. 15-18, Understanding Destiny
vv. 19-22, God's Supreme Judgment
vv. 23-26, Faith in God Holds
vv. 27-28, Conclusion

Compare these verses of song translated by John Wesley with Psalm 73.

Pressing Toward the Mark

I thank thee, uncreated Sun,
  That thy bright beams on me have shined;
I thank thee, who hast overthrown
  My foes, and healed my wounded mind;
I thank thee, whose enlivening voice
Bids my freed heart in thee rejoice.

Uphold me in the doubtful race,
  Nor suffer me again to stray;
Strengthen my feet, with steady pace
  Still to press forward in thy way;
My soul and flesh, O Lord of might,
Fill, satiate, with thy heavenly light.

Thee will I love, my joy, my crown;
  Thee will I love, my Lord, my God;
Thee will I love, beneath thy frown
  Or smile, thy scepter or thy rod.
What though my flesh and heart decay?
Thee shall I love in endless day!

—Johann A. Scheffler

I. The Problem of the Righteous (Read 73:1-3)

Life at times seems like a jigsaw puzzle of pieces to be fitted together. Our view becomes warped if we look only at the pieces without keeping God's design in mind. This mixture of good and evil confuses our choices.

A. God Is Good to the Pure in Heart

1. Do you think faith is more a matter of knowledge or of attitude? _____

2. Why aren't mere facts enough to keep faith firm? _____

9 / THE RIDDLE OF LIFE

B. The Wicked Seem to Prosper
1. Why is it wrong to envy the wicked who prosper? _____

2. How may our faith rise above the problems posed by the success of the ungodly and the hardships of the righteous? _____

II. The Prosperity of the Wicked (Read 73:4-12)
The wicked prosper only in material terms, and this misleading criteria is no true measure.

A. Fosters Pride (vv. 4-6)
1. Circle the following statements true or false.
   - T F The bodies of the wicked are always healthy and strong.
   - T F The wicked are always free from burdens common to mankind.
   - T F Pride breeds violence.

B. Risks Iniquity (vv. 7-12)
1. Circle the statements true or false.
   - T F A heart calloused before God imagines all manner of evil.
   - T F The unchecked wicked scoff and threaten oppression.
   - T F The wicked boast, thinking they are out of God's reach.

The meaning of the Hebrew in verse 10 is uncertain. Moffatt, supported by the RSV, renders it: "So people turn to follow them and see no wrong in them, thinking, 'What does God care?'"

III. Faith's Struggle (Read 73:13-22)
When the wicked prosper, the hopes of the righteous are often stifled. It is hard to believe right will overcome when evil seems to hold sway.

A. Why Bother to Be Good? (vv. 13-16)
1. Does a pure heart bring freedom from suffering?
   a. Sometimes _____ b. Always _____ c. Never _____

2. If the wicked prosper in this life, why should anyone be righteous? _____

3. When should we keep our doubts to ourselves? (v. 15) _____

4. Are the Psalmist's doubts: a. from his ignorance ____ b. due to hasty judgment ____ or, c. because of a defect in God's providence (v. 16) ____?

B. Communion with God (vv. 17-22)

1. Can the intellect solve every problem? Yes ____ No ____

2. How do you think communion with God helps resolve problems with doubts? _____

3. How does the long view of human life help us to resolve the Psalmist's struggle? _____

4. How does verse 20 describe the real quality of a wicked man's prosperity? _____

5. Can you suggest several false hopes for happiness with which friends or neighbors have been led into trouble?

    a. _____
    b. _____
    c. _____

6. List the seeming advantages of the wicked and the prospects of the righteous.

The Wicked	The Righteous
v. 4 _____	v. 1 _____
v. 5 _____	v. 17 _____
v. 12 _____	v. 23 _____

IV. Faith's Triumph (Read 73:23-28)

God's continual presence is life's greatest treasure. The Psalmist joins other Old Testament saints who believed death could not break their communion with God. This passage foreshadows the Christian hope of future life.

A. Faith Trusts the Ever-Present God (vv. 23-26)

1. Faith may be described as my taking hold of God, and God holding on to me. Agree ____ Disagree ____

2. Describe the safety of staying with God (vv. 23-24).

    v. 23a _____
    v. 23b _____
    v. 24a _____
    v. 24b _____

9 / THE RIDDLE OF LIFE

3. What does it mean when the Psalmist speaks of God taking him into glory? _____

4. Why do you think God is both in heaven and on earth? (v. 25)

5. List several aspects of life that are only temporal and several that are eternal.

Temporal	Eternal
a. _____	a. _____
b. _____	b. _____
c. _____	c. _____

6. How does faith help us to rise above human weakness? (v. 26)

7. What does it mean that God can be one's portion forever? (v. 26)

B. Contrasting Destinies (vv. 27-28)

1. When are those who are unfaithful to God destroyed? (v. 27)

2. List some ways the wicked are unfaithful to God.
   a. _____
   b. _____
   c. _____

3. Has the Psalmist gone full circle, ending with the assertion with which he began? (vv. 1, 28) Yes ____ No ____

4. How do I make "the Sovereign Lord" my refuge? _____

5. What has God done for me that makes me want to tell of His deeds? _____

V. Afterglow

1. My integrity wavers when I begin to doubt God's righteousness.
2. This life and the next cannot be separated in God's plan for men.
3. Is my life what I want it to be in the light of God's plan for me?

VI. Prayer Time

When you pray:
1. Meditate on why you first believed God.

2. Focus on God's will for your life instead of on what He allows others to temporarily get away with.

3. Ask God to help you see the long view of life and destiny.

4. Invite four persons to read aloud to the group: Ps. 16:9-11; 17:15; 23:6; 49:15.

5. Praise God for the never-ending joy of His presence.

VII. Some Reflections

1. The Christian's hope for the future life depends on God's life.

2. The nearer we live to God, the less we are troubled by the world's attractions and distractions.

3. God's ways are more appreciated when they are better known.

4. Read Psalm 84 in preparation for the next lesson.

10   Heart Hunger for God's House

PSALM 84

God's house is a place of feasting as well as worship. The fare is food for the spirit.

This psalm, titled "Of the Sons of Korah," is akin to the thought in Psalms 42—43, studied earlier. Few poems in sacred or secular literature equal its depth of feeling and beauty of expression. It has been called one of the sweetest "Psalms of Peace."

Classed as a worship psalm, it is linked with the Feast of Tabernacles observed in the fall. The poem may have been a song chanted by Jewish pilgrims coming for the autumn festival, and refreshed by some verdant valley following the long, dry summer. In the Old Testament, material wealth was considered a sign of divine favor, but the Psalmist knew it is not the sole test. The greatest blessing known to the human heart is communion with God.

The song is in three parts, marked by the occurrence of "Selah," after verses 4 and 8. "Selah" was probably a musical term that meant "pause here." The three stanzas show the progression of the human heart's longing for God. The theme of the first stanza (vv. 1-4) is the heart's desire for God and His house. In the second (vv. 5-8) the subject is the spirit's approach into the Divine Presence. The third stanza (vv. 9-12) celebrates the believer's fellowship with God.

The movement of thought is unbroken. Stanza 2 begins on the same note which ends the first. The prayer begun at the end of stanza 2 continues through the third. The three parts combine as a unit of devotion.

Outline

I. Longing for the Lord's House (84:1-4)
II. The Trusting Heart (84:5-8)
III. Satisfied in God's Presence (84:9-12)

Read Psalm 84 aloud, going around the group. At "Selah," pause and meditate briefly.

This hymn written by Isaac Watts parallels the psalm's message.

Joy of Public Worship

1. *Great God, attend, while Zion sings*
   The joy that from thy presence springs;
   To spend one day with thee on earth
   Exceeds a thousand days of mirth.

3. *God is our sun, he makes our day;*
   God is our shield, he guards our way
   From all assaults of hell and sin,
   From foes without, and foes within.

5. *O God, our King, whose sovereign sway*
   The glorious hosts of heaven obey,
   And devils at thy presence flee;
   Blest is the man that trusts in thee.

I. Longing for the Lord's House (Read 84:1-4)

The very thought of the house of worship stirs the poet's heart. Every part of the sanctuary, from the outer courts to the altar, is hallowed by God's majesty. The presence of the living God is the heart's supreme desire. There one finds true satisfaction of spirit.

A. A True Worshiper Yearns (vv. 1-2)

1. What three words in verse 2 suggest the longing of the total person for God?

   a. _____

   b. _____

   c. _____

2. What made the Temple so attractive to the Psalmist? _____

3. What outward worship aids help a Christian's inner communion with God?

   a. _____

   b. _____

   c. _____

10 / HEART HUNGER FOR GOD'S HOUSE

4. The Psalmist recognized God's presence in His house. Name some other places where you have found Him.
   a. _____
   b. _____
5. What makes the church sanctuary special to you? _____

B. A True Worshiper Praises (vv. 3-4)

1. What need of the worshiper is reflected by nesting birds in the Temple grounds? _____
2. In verse 4, how would you define the word "blessed"? _____
3. How do worshipers today praise God in His house? _____

Selah—"Pause and Meditate"

II. The Trusting Heart (Read 84:5-8)

Though still en route to the sanctuary, the poet foresees the pilgrimage ending in the house of the Lord. Coming in hope and holy expectation, the pilgrims forget the dry and rugged path. With renewed strength they look forward to worshiping God in His sanctuary.

A. The Worshiper Loves God's Way (vv. 5-6)

James Moffatt translates verse 5: "Happy are they who, nerved by thee, set out on pilgrimage!"

1. Note some moods that could unnerve us on a pilgrimage:
   a. Loneliness
   b. _____
   c. _____
2. What journey occupies Christians? Do you recall the title of John Bunyan's famous book? _____

3. How does one draw strength from God through faithful church attendance? _____
4. The "Valley of Baca" (v. 6) means "valley of weeping." It is not a geographic location, but rather a figure of speech like a "well of joy."

Share with the group how God has turned some sorrow of yours into joy.

B. Triumphs over Circumstances (vv. 7-8)
   1. What do you think it means to "go from strength to strength"? _____

   2. Ask one member to read aloud verse 7. Ask a second member to read aloud Isa. 40:31.

   3. How may pain, sorrow, and disappointment become stepping-stones to God? _____

   4. When may we expect God to listen to our prayers, as in verse 8? _____

Selah—"Pause and Meditate"

III. Satisfied in God's Presence (Read 84:9-12)

The blessings of God's house come from the comfort of His presence. Without Him, worship becomes a futile exercise, and His house loses its glory.

A. God's Anointing (vv. 9-10)
   1. Old Testament prophets, priests, and kings were anointed for office. Who do you think is the anointed one spoken of in verse 9? _____ Why? _____

   2. Do you think it is permissible to spiritualize the anointing and consider it a prayer for a personal blessing? Yes _____ No _____ Why? _____

   3. How much better is God's house than the best of the secular world? _____

   4. What position in the church today would be comparable to the doorkeeper of verse 10? _____

   5. What modern phrase would be used to describe "tents of the wicked"? _____

B. God's Protection (vv. 11-12)
   1. Verse 11 is one of two scriptures that calls God a "sun" (cf. Mal. 4:2).
   2. Name some ways the Lord God is a sun to our lives.
      a. _____
      b. _____
      c. _____
   3. How is God our shield? (Cf. Ps. 3:3.) _____

10 / HEART HUNGER FOR GOD'S HOUSE

4. "Favor and honor" (NIV) and "grace and glory" (KJV) are couplets that must follow that order. How would you define favor and grace? _____ How would you define honor and glory?

5. What reward does the Bible promise to us if we walk blamelessly before God? _____

6. Write out the three "blesseds" of worship in this psalm.
   v. 4 _____
   v. 5 _____
   v. 12 _____

IV. Afterglow

1. A holy appetite is a better call to worship than chiming bells.

2. Think how God gives *all* good things—there is *no* good apart from Him. Read in unison Jas. 1:16-17.

3. Our confidence in God depends on our walk with Him in truth and holiness.

V. Prayer Time

When you pray:

1. Expect the reality of God's presence.
2. Hunger and thirst after His righteousness.
3. Express your intention to do His will.
4. Thank God for the light of His truth and the shelter of His glory.
5. Pray for the continued spiritual progress of each member of your group.

VI. Some Reflections

1. When the Lord is our God, both His house and His fellowship are precious.

2. The Psalmist's longing for the Lord's house relates to the Christian's desire to be like Jesus.

3. True worship is not sterile—it produces godly lives.

4. For next week, read Psalm 91 and memorize a favorite verse or verses.

11 Refuge for the Trusting Heart

PSALM 91

Threatened children most often run to the arms of Mom or Dad. But in adult years God is our only "ever-present" refuge.

In this psalm an unknown writer proclaims the theme of trusting God. That theme climaxes in Paul's New Testament exclamation, "If God is for us, who can be against us?" (Rom. 8:31).

Book IV includes Psalms 90—106, a group of miscellaneous poems. Among these, Psalms 90, 91, and 92 form a trilogy of trust. Psalm 90 pleads for deliverance; Psalm 91 offers prayer that trusts God for an answer; and Psalm 92 rejoices in the mighty works of the Lord.

The connection of Psalms 90 and 91 stems from their obvious reference to Deut. 33:27: "The eternal God is your refuge, and underneath are the everlasting arms." Psalm 90 relies on the first position; Psalm 91 expands the second part.

A striking feature of Psalm 91 is that several voices speak. In verses 3-9a and 10-13, the second person, "you," is addressed. In verses 2 and 9b, someone speaks in the first person: "I," "my." In verses 14-16 God speaks in the third person; the one blessed is spoken of as "he" and "him."

The Psalmist expresses personal trust and then encourages Israel's faith. Because of his own steadfast faith, he can comfort God's people. When a nation trusts God, He will deliver and honor it. What is true of the trusting nation also applies to the trusting individual.

Psalm 91, like Psalm 23, pictures Jehovah and the saint in loving fellowship. The saint is with his God and Protector, both in bright and dark days, in joy and in sorrow, in danger and in repose.

Outline
I. A Fervent Trust (91:1-8)
II. Dwelling in Order to Triumph (91:9-13)
III. A Sure Promise (91:14-16)

11 / REFUGE FOR THE TRUSTING HEART

Read verse 1 aloud in unison. The leader may then read verse 2, as the voice of the Psalmist. The chorus responds, reading verses 3-8. The leader replies, as the Psalmist, reading verse 9. The chorus answers, reading verses 10-13. All join in reading the words of God in verses 14-16.

Henry F. Lyte wrote the following hymn based on Psalm 91.

The Sure Refuge

There is a safe and secret place
  Beneath the wings divine,
Reserved for all the heirs of grace;
  O be that refuge mine!

The least and feeblest there may 'bide,
  Uninjured and unawed;
While thousands fall on every side,
  He rests secure in God.

The angels watch him on his way,
  And aid with friendly arm;
And Satan, roaring for his prey,
  May hate, but cannot harm.

He feeds in pastures large and fair
  Of love and truth divine:
O child of God, O glory's heir,
  How rich a lot is thine!

A hand almighty to defend,
  An ear for every call,
An honored life, a peaceful end,
  And heaven to crown it all!

The group may want to sing a verse and chorus of "Leaning on the Everlasting Arms" (*Worship in Song*, no. 446).

I. A Fervent Trust (Read 91:1-8)

Every child of God seeks the inner sanctuary and the mercy seat, but some miss the most holy place because of faulty trust. However, all who respond to God's revelation and abide in faith find this refuge.

A. Confidence in God's Shelter (vv. 1-2)

1. In verse 1, what two titles describe God as supreme?

a. _____
b. _____

2. How would you describe God's shelter, where we can abide? ___
_____

3. In verse 2 what words does the Psalmist use to describe the shelter?
a. _____
b. _____
c. _____

4. Does the Psalmist allude to God's security beyond the pilgrim's visit to the Temple? (Cf. v. 3.) Yes ___ No ___

5. Does God's presence afford shelter today regardless of locality? Yes ___ No ___

6. Let one member read the prayer of Ps. 17:8. Let the group reply by reading in unison 91:1, 4.

7. Circle the following statements true or false.
T F The Psalms often uses "my refuge" to describe God as Protector.
T F The term "my fortress" means "my refuge."
T F "My God" confidently addresses Him whose very name is sacred.

B. Divine Deliverance (vv. 3-8)

1. Give the two images used in verse 3 that refer to hidden danger.
a. _____
b. _____

2. What does the mother bird illustrate in verse 4? _____
For further uses of this figure have two members read aloud Deut. 32:11 and Matt. 23:37.

3. In verse 4b what two words picture God's protection?
a. _____
b. _____

4. Does verse 5 refer to dangers from men? Yes ___ No ___ What dangers are pointed out in verse 6? _____
Name some modern dangers that may occur:

In the daytime	At night
a. _____	a. _____
b. _____	b. _____

11 / REFUGE FOR THE TRUSTING HEART

5. Verses 7 and 8 are understood to refer especially to Israel's sojourn in Egypt. Does verse 7 always apply to God's people? Yes ____ No ____ Does verse 8 always apply to God's people? Yes ____ No ____

II. Dwelling in Order to Triumph (Read 91:9-13)

Those who abide in trust experience triumph. Persistent faith in God overcomes all foes.

A. With God (vv. 9-10)

1. Verses 9 and 10 restate the truth of verses 1-3. Which statement do you like better? _____

2. From your experience, can you recall an occasion when you found the Lord a safe refuge? Yes ____ No ____ If so, be prepared to testify to the group.

3. How do you think personal commitment to God relates to His protection?

B. By Divine Enabling (vv. 11-13)

1. Do you believe in angels? Yes ____ No ____ Why? _____

_____

2. Invite three persons to read aloud these records of angelic care: Gen. 24:7; Dan. 3:28; Heb. 1:13-14.

3. How was the truth of Ps. 91:11-12 misused by Satan in Matt. 4:5-6? _____

4. In verse 13, what four beasts are used to symbolize the powers of evil?
    a. _____ c. _____
    b. _____ d. _____

5. List one or two threatening powers of temptation that God is enabling you to trample.
    a. _____
    b. _____

III. A Sure Promise (Read 91:14-16)

God here pledges himself to the faithful, stating the condition upon which refuge depends.

A. Bond of Love

1. What attitude does God require? _____

2. Verse 14 is rendered: "Because he cleaves to me in love" (RSV). How strong a relationship is indicated? _____

3. What do you think verse 14 means by "because he hath known my name" (KJV), or "for he acknowledges my name" (NIV)? _____

4. Do you think obedience and faith are the natural outflow of God's love in our hearts? Yes _____ No _____ Why? _____

B. Deliverance and Salvation

1. List seven things in verses 14-16 that God promises to do:

   a. _____ e. _____
   b. _____ f. _____
   c. _____ g. _____
   d. _____

2. Give the threefold condition to the promise in verses 14 and 16.

   a. _____
   b. _____
   c. _____

3. Do you think verse 16 refers to: (1) This life _____ (2) Life in heaven _____ (3) Both _____?

4. Jesus' teaching in Matt. 6:33 is anticipated. Yes _____ No _____

IV. Afterglow

1. The more we cling to our Heavenly Father, the more confident we are.
2. Think how God's promises to you are both true and conditional.
3. Psalm 91 strengthens our assurance in Jesus Christ.

V. Prayer Time

When you pray:
1. Rest in the refuge God provides.
2. Claim God's promises as your own.
3. Reaffirm your steadfast love for Him.
4. Believe God for deliverance and everlasting salvation.

VI. Some Reflections

1. Faith produces a positive quality through all of life.
2. Read Psalm 103. Fill your heart and mind with praise to God.

12   A Full Heart Sings Praises

PSALM 103

Imagine David taking up his harp. He sweeps across the strings, striking chords of praise and thanksgiving to God. Believers of all the ages join in chorus.

King David had experienced the mercies of the Lord. He knew the joy of sins forgiven, and marveled at the depth of God's love. Out of these blessings issued this grand outburst of praise and gratitude.

"Praise the Lord, O my soul" is the keynote of the entire psalm. It is a celebration of God's steadfast love for His people.

Later God-fearing kings of Israel also trusted the divine promises. Old Testament saints recited this psalm in their worship, and orthodox Jews still feature it on feast days.

New Testament saints also offered thanksgiving and praise in the words of this Spirit-inspired hymn. Christians across the centuries have received blessing and comfort from its truth.

Beyond its notes of worship, the psalm contains prophetic meaning. A. C. Gaebelein says, "It is the new song which restored and redeemed Israel will sing 'in that day' when their covenant promises are fulfilled" (*The Book of Psalms*, p. 377).

Even now, a glad response of praise wells up from every believer's heart as he thrills to David's song. Worship and adoration of God should not be reserved for special release. They are to burst forth in all of life's seasons.

Outline

    I. A Personal Testimony (103:1-5)
   II. Praise for Past Blessings (103:6-12)
  III. Trust for Present Help (103:13-18)
  IV. The Lord Reigns (103:19-22)

Read the psalm aloud in unison from a common version of the Bible, emphasizing the word "praise" (NIV). Or choose four people to read the four parts of the psalm, using the divisions in the outline above.

Among the many hymns based on Psalm 103 is one by Isaac Watts:

The Tender Mercy of the Lord

O bless the Lord, my soul!
His grace to thee proclaim;
And all that is within me, join
To bless his holy name.

The Lord forgives thy sins,
Prolongs thy feeble breath;
He healeth thine infirmities,
And ransoms thee from death.

He clothes thee with his love,
Upholds thee with his truth;
And like the eagle he renews
The vigor of thy youth.

Then bless his holy name
Whose grace hath made thee whole;
Whose loving-kindness crowns thy days
O bless the Lord, my soul!

I. A Personal Testimony (Read 103:1-5)

True praise to God rises as music from the heart. As with David, our very life and essential self should resound in praise from the depths of our souls.

A. Spiritual Worship (vv. 1-2)

1. What do you think is included in praising God with all our "inmost being"? _____

2. Why do you think the Psalmist dwells upon God's holy name?
_____

3. List five benefits from the Lord.
    a. _____   d. _____
    b. _____   e. _____
    c. _____

B. The Lord Redeems (vv. 3-5)

   1. Under what conditions does God forgive all of our sins? _____
   _____

   2. To what extent may we claim God heals all our diseases? _____
   _____

   3. What three blessings does David recognize in verse 4?

      a. _____
      b. _____
      c. _____

   4. What are some of the good things that God has brought to my life? (v. 5)

      a. _____
      b. _____

II. Praise for Past Blessings (Read 103:6-12)

David's personal experience is confirmed as he recalls God's mercies revealed in history.

A. God's Righteousness (vv. 6-7)

   1. How do you think God works righteousness and justice for the oppressed?

      a. _____
      b. _____

   2. The Psalmist looked back to Moses and God's acts among the children of Israel. What events from your own experience or the experience of your local church remind you of God's mercy? _____
   _____

   3. How was the giving of the law an expression of God's love? (v. 7)
   _____

B. God's Love (vv. 8-12)

   1. From verses 8-10 list some signs of God's love.

      a. _____   d. _____
      b. _____   e. _____
      c. _____   f. _____

   2. Do you think verse 9 is an expression of God's judgment or of His

mercy? _____ How great is God's love for those who trust Him? (v. 11) _____

3. How far is the east from the west? (v. 12) _____

III. Trust for Present Help (Read 103:13-18)

God keeps His covenant with those who fear Him. The Psalmist here contrasts man's immaturity and weakness with God's present help in time of need.

A. As a Father (vv. 13-14)

1. List some words from verses 13-17 that contrast God with man.

God	Man
a. Father	a. Child
b. _____	b. _____
c. _____	c. _____
d. _____	d. _____

B. Those Who Fear God (vv. 15-18)

1. Circle the following statements true or false.
   - T F Fear of God means reverence for His authority.
   - T F God's mercy may be defined as "covenant love."
   - T F Godly fear is one of the first signs of divine life in us.

2. Why is God's love said to be from everlasting to everlasting? ___

IV. The Lord Reigns (Read 103:19-22)

David begins and ends the psalm with a clarion call for praise to the Lord. He opens with the joy of a holy relationship and closes in thankful awe of the Sovereign who rules over all.

A. His Throne

1. In verse 19, does the Psalmist imply that the Lord ruled in his heart before the writing of the psalm? Yes ____ No ____

2. To achieve His own purposes, the Lord must establish His throne in every person's heart. Agree ____ Disagree ____ Why? _____

3. Where does God reign (v. 19)? _____

4. What is the character of His reign? _____

B. His Heavenly Servants

1. Circle the following statements true or false.

    T F Angels are heavenly ministers and messengers.

    T F Angels are said to be mightier than man.

    T F Angels obey God's commands.

2. Why do you think David calls upon the angels to praise God? ____

3. Does the existence of angels show God's personal care for His people? Yes ____ No ____

4. How do you think angels are involved in the government of God's kingdom in world affairs? ____

5. Why is it appropriate for praise to God to be all-encompassing?

V. Afterglow

1. Imagine how David's call to praise unites, as it were, the tender notes of the flute with the ringing tones of the trumpet.

2. Review the circuit of praise in this psalm:

    a. "Praise the Lord, O my soul" (vv. 1-2).

    b. "Praise the Lord, you his angels" (v. 20).

    c. "Praise the Lord, all his heavenly hosts" (v. 21).

    d. "Praise the Lord, all his works" (v. 22).

    e. "Praise the Lord, O my soul" (v. 22)—embracing all creation.

3. Think how the song celebrates the greatness of God.

VI. Prayer Time

When you pray:

1. Praise God for His holiness.
2. Praise God for His mercy and forgiveness.
3. Praise God for His love to all who obey Him.
4. Praise God for His everlasting kingdom.

VII. Some Reflections

1. David's spirit of praise would make a difference in our worship.
2. Read Psalms 121—122; memorize 121.

13 The Traveler's Psalms

PSALMS 121—122

Life is a journey. Our pilgrimage to the heavenly city is like that of the faithful who traveled to Jerusalem to worship.

Book V of the Psalter is both the longest in content and in the number of psalms it contains. It includes Psalms 107—150, and the 44 chapters are divided into four collections. The two we study today come from the second collection, Psalms 120—134, known as "Songs of Ascents."

Psalm 121 breathes a strong and steady trust in God's faithfulness. The poem is the second in a trilogy tracing the Psalmist's ascent from the hardship of exile to the joy of worship in Jerusalem. He rejoices in the One who watches over him throughout the treacherous journey.

The word "keep" characterizes the thought of this psalm. Though partially hidden by translation, the concept occurs six times in the last five verses. This repeated thought pinpoints God's loving care for the individual. God dispels the doubts, fears, and anxieties of faithful travelers because His keeping is "both now and forevermore."

Psalm 122 completes the trilogy begun in 120. The theme is Jerusalem, the Holy City, the Psalmist's pride and joy. After a successful journey from his foreign home, the pilgrim exults at the gates of his beloved city.

Pious and patriotic Jews traveled to Jerusalem for the great festivals three times a year (cf. Deut. 16:16-17). On these journeys the pilgrims faced both dangers and delights. Hearts thrilled when the procession at last came to the Holy City and the Temple itself.

Christians today may read these psalms as speaking to the past, present, and future. The same God who kept the Psalmist keeps us in the way. We experience similar joys of worship, but we now look for the New Jerusalem, whose builder and ruler is God.

Outline
I. The Lord Will Help (121:1-4)

13 / THE TRAVELER'S PSALMS

II. The Lord Will Keep (121:5-8)
III. The Pilgrim's Joy (122:1-2)
IV. The Pilgrim's City (122:3-5)
V. The Pilgrim's Prayer (122:6-9)

Repeat Psalm 121 together from memory.
Charles Wesley wrote a hymn that echoes the message of this psalm.

My Help Cometh from the Lord

To the hills I lift mine eyes,
The everlasting hills;
Streaming thence in fresh supplies,
My soul the Spirit feels:
Will he not his help afford?
Help, while yet I ask, is given:
God comes down; the God and Lord
Who made both earth and heaven.

Faithful soul, pray always; pray,
And still in God confide;
He thy feeble steps shall stay,
Nor suffer thee to slide;
Lean on thy Redeemer's breast;
He thy quiet spirit keeps;
Rest in him, securely rest;
Thy watchman never sleeps.

I. The Lord Will Help (Read 121:1-4)

These verses become more meaningful when the second clause of verse 1 is translated as a question (as in the NIV): "Where does my help come from?" The source of help and safety is not in mountains. The only dependable Helper is the Lord.

A. As Creator (vv. 1-2)

1. Why do you think the Psalmist considered the hills as possible sources of help? _____

2. In what respects is God also the God of the valleys? _____

3. Can you think of some ways people today confuse the worship of creation with worshiping the Creator? _____

B. As Guardian (vv. 3-4)
    1. What does "He will not let your foot slip" mean? (Cf. 1 Cor. 10:13.)
_____

    2. How does God's watch-care over people differ from man's concern (v. 4)? _____

II. The Lord Will Keep (Read 121:5-8)
God's presence brings protection and shelter for His people against every threatening force. He cares for us both by day and night.

A. His Protection (vv. 5-6)
    1. To what extent does God protect our lives from natural forces?
_____

B. His Preserving Presence (vv. 7-8)
    1. List the clauses (vv. 4-8) that speak of God's keeping.
        a. _____ d. _____
        b. _____ e. _____
        c. _____ f. _____

    2. What does "the Lord will watch over your coming and going" mean? _____

    3. Does the expression in verses 7-8 of the Lord's keeping extend to all that man is and does? Yes _____ No _____

    4. Does God ever fail us? Yes _____ No _____

    Invite someone to read aloud Rom. 8:31-39.

III. The Pilgrim's Joy (Read 122:1-2)
Read Psalm 122 responsively, verse by verse, beginning with the leader, then the group. Read the last verse in unison.

This psalm, ascribed to David, reveals a deep love for the worship of the Lord. The king's response is wholehearted.

A. The House of the Lord
    1. How was the joy of the Psalmist in verse 1 twofold? _____
_____

    2. Give some advantages of worshiping with other God-honoring people.
        a. _____

13 / THE TRAVELER'S PSALMS

      b. _____
      c. _____
   3. If we love the Lord, we will love His house. Agree _____ Disagree _____

B. End of the Journey
   1. What was the destination of the pilgrims? _____

   2. Which do you think is greater, the joy of anticipation or the joy of realization? _____

   3. In what way are the gates of Jerusalem and the gates of heaven similar? _____

IV. The Pilgrim's City (Read 122:3-5)

Jerusalem, David's goal, is more wonderful than his dreams. It is "a city solid and unbroken" (Moffatt). This is where "the tribes of the Lord" meet together.

A. Place of Meeting
   1. Give at least three reasons why the tribes meet there.
      a. _____
      b. _____
      c. _____
   2. There is a possible prophetic significance in this psalm about Jerusalem. Ask a member to read aloud Isa. 2:2-3.

B. Place of Praise
   1. How are judgment and justice related to praise? _____

   2. How do you think the judgment and justice of David's throne would be related to the justice of God? _____

V. The Pilgrim's Prayer (Read 122:6-9)

As the site of the Temple, God's house, Jerusalem was a sacred city. David prays for her ongoing peace and prosperity.

A. Peace
   1. How do you think peace was related to the security of Jerusalem?

2. How is our security related to peace in the church? _____

3. According to current events, do you think the prayer for the peace of Jerusalem will ever be answered? Yes _____ No _____ Why? _____

4. Should Christians pray for the peace of Jerusalem along with peace for our churches and nations? Yes _____ No _____ Why? _____

B. Prosperity
1. How does peace affect the prosperity of Jerusalem? _____ _____ Of the Church? _____

2. Do you expect the present city of Jerusalem to prosper? Yes _____ No _____ Why? _____

VI. Afterglow
1. Recall how you have experienced the keeping power of God.
2. Share a recent incident in which you knew God watched over you.

VII. Prayer Time
When you pray:
1. Give thanks to the God of creation.
2. Trust in His keeping power amid all trials and temptations.
3. Commit the unknown to God.
4. Ask for peace in your church.
5. Pray for those in your study group who may have special personal or family needs.

VIII. Some Reflections
1. Our pilgrimage ends at Christ's second coming, or when we meet Him in death.
2. Heaven will be wonderful beyond our expectations, just as Jerusalem exceeded the anticipation of these pilgrims.
3. Read Psalm 139; memorize at least two verses.

14 God, the Searcher of Hearts

PSALM 139

Who knows all the depths of man, his needs, and all his whimsical manners? God, our Maker, does!

The Psalmist here tells the matchless wonders of the Lord. Rabbi Aben Ezra acclaimed this poem "The Crown of All the Psalms." It is in the third collection of Book V, 138—145. Because each psalm has the name of David in the title, this section is called "A Little Davidic Collection."

The psalm, as a poem of trust, has qualities of a hymn, but it is predominantly a personal prayer. David views the omniscience and omnipresence of the Lord, not as formal divine attributes, but as he had verified them in personal experience.

The author's conscience gives him a sense of sin and responsibility. In response he prays to the One who is not only Judge, but Friend. Though God is feared as none else, He is also loved as none else is loved. The Bible here assures us of God's presence, of His all-seeing eye, and of His protecting hand.

Outline
I. Divine Omniscience (139:1-6)
II. Divine Omnipresence (139:7-12)
III. God's Personal Concern (139:13-16)
IV. Divine Providence (139:17-22)
V. The Safeguard of Prayer (139:23-24)

Select individuals to read the scripture portions aloud, as the psalm is divided in the outline above. Then read in unison the hymn of Isaac Watts based on this psalm:

Omniscience

Lord, all I am is known to thee;
  In vain my soul would try
To shun thy presence, or to flee
  The notice of thine eye.

Thy all-surrounding sight surveys
  My rising and my rest,
My public walks, my private ways,
  The secrets of my breast.

My thoughts lie open to thee, Lord,
  Before they're formed within;
And ere my lips pronounce the word,
  Thou knowest the sense I mean.

O wondrous knowledge, deep and high!
  Where can a creature hide?
Within thy circling arms I lie,
  Beset on every side.

I. Divine Omniscience (Read 139:1-6)

In Gen. 16:13, Hagar recognized the Lord as "the God who sees me." A thousand years later the Psalmist is awed that God knows all about him. And today, wonder of wonders, God knows our 20th-century concerns.

A. God Knows All (vv. 1-5)

1. Circle the following statements true or false.

    T F God's searching tells of His penetrating knowledge.

    T F We can hide our thoughts from God.

    T F God scans our whole lives—knowing every thought and action.

2. How do you think God hems us in with His knowledge? (v. 5)

B. Beyond Human Understanding (v. 6)

1. Wisdom means to make good judgments on the basis of adequate knowledge. Based on this truth, why does God's wisdom surpass ours?

14 / GOD, THE SEARCHER OF HEARTS

2. List several things that God knows about you that are not now known to you.

a. _____ c. _____

b. _____ d. _____

II. Divine Omnipresence (Read 139:7-12)

The all-knowing God is everywhere present. When I sin, there is no hiding from His presence. But also when I serve Him, His Spirit is present to support and help me throughout time and eternity.

A. All-pervading (vv. 7-11)

1. List places that are difficult for men to reach but where God's Spirit is easily present.

v. 8a _____

v. 8b _____

vv. 9-10 _____

v. 11 _____

2. What is the meaning of "if I make my bed in the depths" (v. 8)? Look up the meaning of the Hebrew word *sheol*.

B. Purposeful Presence (vv. 10-12)

1. What does verse 10 tell about God's presence and purpose? _____
_____

2. Do you think God's presence in all things is purposeful or accidental? _____

III. God's Personal Concern (Read 139:13-16)

Even with scant scientific knowledge, the Psalmist knew the all-knowing God was concerned with every detail of his life. Amazingly, His interest began when we were conceived, and His plan for our lives goes back to the creation of man.

A. Before Birth (v. 13)

1. Ask a member to read aloud Job 10:8-12. Note how Job pleads God's role as Creator as the basis of his prayer for protection.

2. If God is involved in our formation, how do you explain birth defects? _____

B. Guidance in Life (vv. 14-16)

1. Name some ways in which we are "fearfully and wonderfully made" (v. 14). If some member is familiar with biological science, let him explain the laws of inheritance through the genes in the sperm and ovum.

2. In what way do you think God ordains all our days? (v. 16) To what extent do we ourselves determine our destinies? _____

IV. Divine Providence (Read 139:17-22)

Aware of God's all-pervading presence, David believes His will is good and perfect. He is thus assured of God's unfailing care.

A. God's Thoughts (vv. 17-18)

1. Circle the following statements true or false.

   T F God's thoughts are precious because He thinks about us.
   T F The divine thought includes all creation.
   T F God's salvation and presence are for whosoever will.

2. Why cannot sleep or death separate the trusting soul from God? (v. 17) _____

Read in unison David's doxology, verses 17-18. Then let a member read aloud Paul's doxology in Rom. 11:33-36.

B. God's Protection and Punishment (vv. 19-22)

1. The divine providence that protects the righteous will ultimately destroy the wicked. Agree _____ Disagree _____

2. Circle the following statements true or false.

   T F A sense of God's holiness results in knowing the awfulness of sin.
   T F The enemies of God are also the enemies of God's people.
   T F To love righteousness is to hate evil.

V. A Safeguard of Prayer (Read 139:23-24)

Knowing that none can escape God's judgment, we find ourselves in the beam of His searchlight. Rather than try to evade the eye of God, we should expose ourselves in prayer.

A. Kept from the Wicked Way

1. Write out the fourfold petition of verses 23-24.

   v. 23a _____

14 / GOD, THE SEARCHER OF HEARTS

      v. 23b _____
      v. 24a _____
      v. 24b _____

    2. Why do you think the Psalmist prayed, "Search me, O God," when he had already said, "O Lord, you have searched me" (v. 1)? _____

    3. Do you think David suspected actual wickedness in his spirit, or did he pray to overcome weakness and carelessness? _____

    4. To what areas of life did David refer when he spoke of the following:
My heart _____
My thoughts _____
My way _____

B. Led in the Way Everlasting
    1. Discuss how openness to God allows Him to lead us in His way.

    2. How deeply am I engaged in God's plans for the redemption of the world? *(a)* Little _____ *(b)* Somewhat _____ *(c)* All He has shown me _____

VI. Afterglow
    1. God's searchings are as a beacon at an airport, to keep the pilots on course.

    2. Sing verse 1 of "Cleanse Me" (*Worship in Song*, no. 297).

VII. Prayer Time
When you pray:
1. Ask God to search your own heart.
2. Let Him try you and mold your thoughts.
3. Pray for His guidance daily for each member of your group.
4. Thank Him for His loving protection.

VIII. Some Reflections
    1. God's searchings are less painful than His judgment of wickedness.

    2. Salvation requires the discovery of evil in our lives and an effectual deliverance from it.

    3. Read Psalms 148; 149; and 150 to prepare for the final lesson. Give praise to the Lord with a life of devotion and service.

15 Praise the Lord

PSALMS 148; 149; 150

Release your faith in fullest praise. Open your heart to allow a bubbling overflow in gratitude to God for all He has done.

The last of the four minor collections in Book V, Psalms 146—150, is known as "The Great Hallel." These praise hymns have been used daily in the morning synagogue service of Jewish worship from very early times. "Hallelujah" *(Hallelu-Yah)* is the Hebrew for "Praise the Lord!"

This praise is not because of God's help for His servants. It is directly and personally for Him. God is worthy of all possible praise. Let us sound it forth in full volume—from our hearts.

Imagine that the Psalmist has changed instruments. Instead of strumming the harp, he now blows the trumpet. With tremendous force, the notes of praise sound forth in repeated blasts.

Outline
I. Praise from the Heavens and the Earth (148:1-14)
II. Praise for Salvation and Vindication (149:1-9)
III. Triumphant Symphony (150:1-6)

Divide the group into two choruses; read the psalms aloud as follows:
First chorus—Ps. 148:1-4
Second chorus—vv. 5-6
First chorus—vv. 7-12
Second chorus—vv. 13-14
First chorus—Ps. 149:1-3
Second chorus—v. 4
First chorus—vv. 5-6
Second chorus—vv. 7-9
Full chorus—Ps. 150:1a—"Praise the Lord."
First chorus—"Praise God in his sanctuary."

Second chorus—"Praise him in his mighty heavens."
First chorus—"Praise him for his acts of power."
Second chorus—"Praise him for his surpassing greatness."
First chorus—"Praise him with the sounding of the trumpet."
Second chorus—"Praise him with the harp and lyre."
First chorus—"Praise him with tambourine and dancing."
Second chorus—"Praise him with the strings and flute."
First chorus—"Praise him with the clash of cymbals."
Second chorus—"Praise him with resounding cymbals."
Full chorus—"Let everything that has breath praise the Lord. Hallelujah!"

I. Praise from the Heavens and Earth (Read 148:1-14)

This psalm reflects an orderly structure of worship, calling upon the heavens and then the earth to praise the Lord. It is the biblical base for William J. Kirkpatrick's gospel hymn, "Hallelujah, Praise Jehovah!" (*Praise and Worship* hymnal, no. 373).

> *Hallelujah, praise Jehovah!*
> *From the heavens praise His name.*
> *Praise Jehovah in the highest;*
> *All His angels, praise proclaim.*
> *All His hosts, together praise Him—*
> *Sun, and moon, and stars on high.*
> *Praise Him, O ye heav'n of heavens,*
> *And ye floods above the sky.*

A. From the Heavens (vv. 1-6)

1. List the "Praise the Lords" in vv. 2-4, calling for God's praise from the heavens.

v. 2 _____   v. 4 _____
v. 2 _____   v. 4 _____
v. 3 _____
v. 3 _____
v. 3 _____

2. On what is the call to praise based? (vv. 5-6) _____

3. Throughout Scripture, God's spoken word calls the finite universe into being. Read aloud Gen. 1:3-5, and Heb. 11:3.
Stanza 2 of Kirkpatrick's hymn declares:

> *Let them praises give Jehovah;*
> *They were made at His command.*
> *Them forever He established;*
> *His decree shall ever stand.*

B. From the Earth (vv. 7-14)

1. List the things from earth that are called to join in praise (vv. 7-10).

v. 7 _____ v. 8 _____ v. 9 _____
v. 7 _____ v. 8 _____ v. 10 _____
v. 8 _____ v. 9 _____ v. 10 _____
v. 8 _____ v. 9 _____ v. 10 _____
v. 8 _____ v. 9 _____ v. 10 _____

2. From verses 11-12 list the classes and ages of men summoned to praise God.

v. 11 _____ v. 11 _____ v. 12 _____
v. 11 _____ v. 12 _____ v. 12 _____
v. 11 _____ v. 12 _____

3. Stanza 2 of "Hallelujah, Praise Jehovah!" continues:

> *From the earth, oh, praise Jehovah,*
> *All ye floods, ye dragons all;*
> *Fire, and hail, and snow, and vapors,*
> *Stormy winds that hear Him call.*

Verse 3 follows:

> *All ye fruitful trees and cedars,*
> *All ye hills and mountains high,*
> *Creeping things and beasts and cattle,*
> *Birds that in the heavens fly;*
> *Kings of earth and all ye people,*
> *Princes great, earth's judges all;*
> *Praise His name, young men and maidens,*
> *Aged men, and children small.*

4. List three reasons why the Lord is worthy to be praised.
   a. _____
   b. _____
   c. _____

5. What is the meaning of the term "horn" in verse 14? (See the footnote in NIV.) _____
What kind of strength does God give us today? _____

II. Praise for Salvation and Vindication (Read 149:1-9)

Here are two contrasting moods, (1) people rejoicing in their Maker, and (2) thanksgiving for God's judgment against their enemies. Israel is favored with divine blessing and deliverance. She praises the Lord for saving her people from sin and distress.

A. Praise for Salvation (vv. 1-5)

1. For a parallel song of praise, read aloud Zeph. 3:14-17.

2. Why do you think the Psalmist calls for a "new song" of praise to the Lord? _____

3. What is the New Testament and the modern-day equivalent of "the assembly of the saints" (v. 1)? _____

4. What cause has Israel to rejoice in God? (v. 4) _____

5. How did Israel express her praise to God?

   v. 3 _____   v. 3 _____
   v. 3 _____   v. 5 _____

B. Praise for Vindication (vv. 6-9)

1. Circle the following statements true or false.

   T F The godly praise God for salvation and deliverance.

   T F The saints sing where they once wept during oppression.

2. This passage was used as a national hymn which looked to the future when Israel would be an instrument of divine justice.

3. What is the meaning of God's "double-edged sword in their hands"? (Cf. Heb. 4:12.) _____

4. What do you understand verses 7-9 tell us about the glory of God's saints? _____

5. When do you think true peace will come to this world? _____

III. Triumphant Symphony (Read 150:1-6)

This poem is a fitting doxology for the whole Book of Psalms. It was probably written for that very purpose. The concept of praise reminds us of the declaration at Jesus' birth, "Glory to God in the highest" (Luke 2:14). It anticipates the triumph of His second coming when He shall reign as "King of kings and Lord of lords" (Rev. 19:16).

A. Call to Praise (vv. 1-2)
   1. Why do you think praise should begin in God's sanctuary? _____

   2. Recall some of God's acts of power.
      a. _____
      b. _____
      c. _____

   3. Why must our praise to God include both His goodness and His power? _____

   4. Could we worship a God who was good but not powerful? Yes ____ No ____ Could we worship Him if He were powerful but not good? Yes ____ No ____

B. Instruments of Praise (vv. 3-6)
   1. List the musical instruments mentioned in verses 3-5.

   v. 3 _____   v. 4 _____
   v. 3 _____   v. 4 _____
   v. 3 _____   v. 5 _____
   v. 4 _____

   2. If I cannot play an instrument, am I excused from praising God? (v. 6) _____

   3. This psalm may reflect the result of a devout life, the glorious end for those who are faithful in this world. Agree ____ Disagree ____

IV. Afterglow
   1. Is my praise life to God as full as He deserves?

   2. How can I become more mindful of giving heartfelt praise to God in every circumstance?

V. Prayer Time
   When you pray:
   1. Praise God, your Creator.
   2. Praise God, your Savior.
   3. Praise God for present victory and future triumph.
   4. Praise God, your eternal Lord and King.
   5. Praise God for His presence during your study of the Psalms. Praise Him for the new friends you have made.

VI. Some Reflections

Sing the Doxology:

> *Praise God, from whom all blessings flow;*
> *Praise Him, all creatures here below;*
> *Praise Him above, ye heav'nly host.*
> *Praise Father, Son, and Holy Ghost.*
> *Amen.*

Bibliography

Beacon Bible Commentary, vol. 3. Kansas City: Beacon Hill Press of Kansas City, 1967.
Gaebelein, Arno C. *The Book of the Psalms.* New York: "Our Hope" Publications, 1939.
Gray, James M. *Christian Worker's Commentary.* New York: Fleming H. Revell Co., 1915.
Hymnal of the Methodist Episcopal Church. New York: Nelson and Phillips, 1878.
Praise and Worship, Hymnal. Kansas City: Nazarene Publishing House, n.d.
Scroggie, Graham W. *The Psalter.* 3 vols. New York: Harper and Brothers, n.d.
Spurgeon, Charles H. *Great Verses from the Psalms.* Edited by Norman Hillyer. Grand Rapids: Zondervan Publishing House, 1977.
Wesley, John. *Explanatory Notes upon the Old Testament*, vol. 2. Reprint. Salem, Ohio: Schmul Publishers, 1975.
Worship in Song, Hymnal. Kansas City: Lillenas Publishing Co., 1972.

For information about additional Beacon Hill Press of Kansas City individual or small-group Bible study guides, contact your local bookstore or write directly to the publisher,

Beacon Hill Press of Kansas City, MO 64141-0527